The BEST of
BOTH WORLDS

Sangeeta Bhalla

To order additional copies of this book, contact:
Xlibris LLC
0-800-056-3182
www.xlibrispublishing.co.uk
orders@xlibrispublishing.co.uk
517326

CONTENTS

DEDICATION

Dedicating a book of thoughts to my father and my best friend Rajesh, who has always been there for me since I was a child where I first held his finger to take my first step, up until now where I have matured into an independent women. I love you Dad and Mum.

ACKNOWLEDGEMENT

I owe my loving thanks to my family and friends. There endless words of encouragement and enthusiasm made it possible for me to complete this book. I am thankful to the members of the South Asian society and those individuals on Facebook for participating in my research study. Finally I would like to thank the following people for their contribution: Deepak Badlani, Omar Ishaq, Danny Clarke, Sonia and Gaurav Patel, Rhiann pryor, Marie Terrase Png, Anita and Hiten Rajguru, Uhuru Robinson, Sonya and Sandeep Varaich. And most importantly god for giving me a good head on my shoulders.

CHAPTER 1

Introduction:

South Asians undergo additional sources of stress due to migration and 'culture clash' (clash in values, beliefs, and traditions between the Asian and Western cultures). Some fail to get the appropriate help as their cultural background is not understood, while others find it hard keeping a balance between the Western and Eastern values. This book outlines a research study exploring the perceptions of stress re: family and lifestyle amongst South Asian parents living in England (first generation) and their children (second generation) who are either born or brought up in England. My aims to capture South Asians' insight on the notions of stress in the context of cultural migration and family dynamics.

Importance of Culture in Health

Culture can be defined as a learnt set of shared perceptions about individual's beliefs, values, and norms. Each culture has its own principles that can generate one's self-concept (how to act in relation to others/environment). Such principles within different cultures will have different effects on the individual's health behaviour e.g. impact on physical, psychological, and social health. Understanding culture is important in understanding individuals. Culture determines how we define, think about, and understand health (Lustig & Koester, 1996). Thus the need to consider the role of culture in health promotion is essential.

Individualism versus Collectivism

Cultural differences in self-concepts have given rise to terms such as individualism and collectivism (Markus and Kitayama, 1991). Most Western nations operate within individualistic cultures whereas Eastern nations have a more collectivist orientation (Trafmow, Triandis and Gotto, 1991). In an individualistic culture, children from a young age are brought up with values of having independent thinking and being successful for themselves. Their main goal in life is to become self-reliant, achieve self-knowledge, and realise one's capability (Schoeneman, 1997).

The collectivist culture on the other hand prompts an individual's behaviour and the way they think towards their family as well as their extended family. Success in their life is seen as 'Bringing honour and glory to the family' (Ghuman, 1999). They are brought up to make personal sacrifices in order to support their immediate and extended families (Shaw, 1988).

The upbringing in collectivist cultures is for them to be respectful and obedient towards their elders and be interdependent. They refer to themselves as a community because their identity is made up from others. The perception of others within the community is highly regarded. Collectivists do not discriminate between personal and public roles, as they let go of their personal goals for the benefit of the group. There is a lot of emphasis put on the concern and need for others (Schoeneman, 1997).

Individuals do not have control over a situation due to social and environmental factors. However, culture is another factor that reduces the level of control an individual has. In individualistic societies, the individual is more likely to have control as they are given the independence of influencing or changing existing situations. Whereas collectivists lack independent control, as it belongs to the social or the personal system to which they belong to.

By contrast, individualistic cultures are based on emotionally detached relationships and are concerned with equal benefits (Schoeneman, 1997). From an individualist's perspective, society is a large network consisting of people. Those people who accept social organisation have limited control thus limited freedom (Schoeneman, 1997).

The differences in perception between individualistic and collectivistic cultures also affect the way in which individuals perceive intimacy and love. Within the individualistic culture, it is natural for individuals to meet, fall in love, live together, and then get married. However, within the Asian culture, marriage is based on the decisions made by family members; hence arranged marriages are not seen as unusual. Marriages within the Asian culture are dependent on factors such as occupation and social status rather than love and intimacy in comparison with the Western culture (Dion and Dion, 1993). Furthermore, subject matters such as premarital sex (Delphy and Lenord, 1992), divorce (Anwar, 1998), and dating (Ghuman, 1991) are taboo within the Asian culture but accepted within the Western culture.

First generation South Asians

First generation South Asians in India, Pakistan or Bangladesh were bought up on the collectivist values of interdependence, male dominance over female and personal sacrifice for their families. Their choices regarding education and marriage were dictated by their elders including immediate, extended family and their community. During this period love marriages were rare, children lived with their parents and women when married (same religion and caste) lived with their in laws. TV programmes and movies portrayed the reserved culture which was a characteristic feature of the South Asian culture. Movies showed subtle intimacy scenes where birds flying or two flowers touching would symbolise sexual characteristics/intimacy and love. Subject matters within the media such as divorce and premarital sex were seen as taboo. Fashion embraced the South Asian reserved culture with Indian Sari's and Indian suits with little flesh showing.

Migrating to England, first generation South Asians wanted to uphold their beliefs and values and pass them down to their children. However migrating to a country which differed in lifestyle, values and beliefs was not easy for them. Research indicates that 89% South Asian women who were immigrants committed suicide. One may assume that this may be because of the several issues that individuals undergo when migrating, such as a sense of loss and isolation especially when the person has difficulty with the English language, which could be a precursor of stress.

Another possibility is because of the conflict between the expectations of family and community, hence Asian individuals find it difficult in keeping a balance between the Asian and Western cultures. Further support is provided by a large number of Asian women finding it difficult to balance the role of the family as well as a successful career (Burningham, 2001).

Furthermore, a study conducted in Birmingham looked at the suicidal cases of individuals admitted in a hospital following attempted suicide over a two-year period. Findings conclude that South Asian females were twice more likely to be admitted in hospital due to the attempts of suicide than their Caucasian counterparts. A reason for such behaviour was because of the marital problems that these women experienced. The cause of the marital problems was because of the arranged marriages leading to clash in views. When interviewed about their cultural identity and life events, some of the

South Asian women who had attempted suicide showed that 'culture clash' was the main problem. This shows us that in addition to the Asian youth, some older Asian females also experience the stress that arises due to the 'culture clash' (Assisi, n.d.).

Overall mental distress amongst Asian women has been a cause of concern. Suicide rates amongst Asian women between the ages fifteen and thirty-five living in Britain were twice the national average for all young women of that age. The reason for such striking statistics has come down to Asian women failing to get the appropriate help, as there is a lack of understanding of the Asian women's background and their individual needs (Burningham, 2001).

Second generation South Asians

During the period when the first generation South Asians had their children, the western influences such as changes in lifestyle had an impact on the traditional ways of life in South Asian nations. This was and still is emphasised by the media e.g. TV programmes, films, magazines as well as the environment in which South Asians live in (multi-ethnic society within the western culture). For example TV programmes now show teenagers dating, kissing scenes, or adults (over 24 years old) living independently and not with their families. According to the second generation South Asians these seem to be the norms as they know no different. However this was not the case for first generation South Asian when they viewed their Asian programmes.

Due to these changes, many second generation South Asians want to have fewer restrictions, adapt to the independent culture and want to have the freedom of making their own choices within their life rather than being told that is what they have to or will do. Some feel that they want to be trusted more; they want their lifestyle but not a bad name to shame their parents. Many do not agree with certain family morals as they may be stressful due to what they perceive around them in the Western nation. These include not dating before marriage; interracial relationships, everything done should be obeyed by immediate and extended family, being interdependent, parental pressure on education, and differences in socialisation/lifestyle. Thus this led to the South Asian family structure taking most of the strain. Second generation South Asians feel that they trying to find a balance between the two differing principle systems is stressful and one cannot be his/her own self (Ghuman, 1991).

Furthermore, it is not surprising that South Asian individuals want to adapt to some of the individualistic entities, specifically young adults, as they are exposed to the westernisation and urbanisation. One can also presume that being educated in the Western culture can also play a vital role, leading young South Asians to shift their self-concepts from collectivism to individualism (Schoeneman, 1994).

There have been several challenges that ethnic minority parents face when bringing up their children in the Western nation in the twenty-first century. Living between two different cultures which is the British way of life and one's collectivist culture proposed by one's family can be a very rich and a demanding experience. There are a lot of conflicts and challenges that arise through this, which are due to religion, beliefs, values, and traditions that can influence family dynamics (Ghuman, 1999).

Within the western nation individuals in their youth learn to pull away from their parents to achieve independence in order to search for their self-identity, experiment with their sexuality, and open up to personal relationships. They also make vital choices concerning their subjects to study and pursuing their professional occupation. South Asians share some of these concerns within their youth. Nevertheless, growing up in a fast-changing Western society and being bounded with collectivist values from their parents, they undergo additional problems. It is important to understand that their socialisation is different in comparison to their parents, as they are trying to understand and deal with the demands and expectations from individualistic and collectivist cultures (Ghuman, 1991).

At adolescence, individuals ask several questions such as 'Who am I?' to explore their self-identity, but those young adults from immigrant families ask to which community they belong to, trying to find their place within the Western society as new members. Back home these children are often referred to as 'British born confused Desi'.

This is because when going to their back home countries, many south Asians refer to them as 'gore' (Caucasians) as they are living in England, but back in England they are referred to as Indian or Pakistani's. Thus many South Asians seek for belongingness.

Asian immigrants' shame-based culture may be one of the reasons why Asian parents may be putting strict expectations and restrictions on their children, as they are concerned about the perceptions of others within the community 'what will people say back home or within the community' (Anwar, 1998). For example a family would only approve of their significant others adapting to some of the elements of the western lifestyle, if it has been allowed or followed by their extended family. This allows for the blame to be passed onto others if ever questioned. Due to strict expectations that they place on their children, Asian children feel that their ambitions are not theirs but their parents.

This is further supported by Radhakrishna and Chan (1997), who carried out an experiment in which respondents were given ten objectives that were put forward by their parents as well as the objectives they set themselves. They were then asked to rank the objectives in order of importance. Indians ranked their parents and their aspirations paying the same importance. However, the Americans saw their objectives more important than their parents.

Furthermore, health and social workers say rates of depression are high amongst Asian youths, and in some cases, this results in suicide. Health professionals need to be aware of the influence of the intense academic pressure and strict parenting on Asian youth. This is because these factors tend to contribute to high rates of depression amongst young Asians. Recent cases of suicidal attempts amongst the young Asians have been attributed to the conflict between family and community clash of ideas. This is because the Asian youth find it difficult to keep a balance between the collectivist and individualistic cultures (Assisi, n.d.).

South Asian culture within the Western nation

Once in London there were no South Asians or black individuals patrolling the street, no ethnic minority were MP's, South Asian or black individual rarely appeared in Movies or TV programmes and within schools there were 50 Caucasians in relation to one South Asian. Many South Asians also faced a lot of bullying and Racism as they were viewed as different; the way they dressed, spoke and looked. In London there was a sense of conformity where everyone spoke and dressed the same way. In 1976 Gurdip Singh Chaggar aged 18 was stabbed by a gang of Caucasian individuals in a racist attack. Many South Asians feared the skinheads who bullied the South Asians with their constant assaults. This partly gave rise to the anti-racist demonstration which was held in Southall. However this demonstration tuned into riots with many being injured, arrested and a New Zealand teacher Blair Peach was killed by being fatally assaulted by the police. Many South Asians felt a loss in belongingness being the minority yearning for their culture back home.

Now South Asians have become the second largest population in the UK have influenced the western culture through the development of many Indian restaurants, their bhangra music (shown on TV programmes e.g. Britain's got talent and recently in the Olympics 2012), instruments (used by many UK artists creating a mixture of genre), and South Asian artists (who have reached mainstream success e.g. Apache Indian, Punjabi Mc and Rishi Rich). Furthermore many South Asians have attracted multi-ethnic audiences through the media and cinema (movies such as Bend it like Beckam, American Desi, East is East, Pink Panther and TV programmes such as Goodness Gracious Me and taking part in the popular TV programme Eastenders).

The popularity of the British Pakistani boxer Amir Khan and the business tycoon man Lakshmi Mittal (currently Britain's richest man and the fifth richest man in the world) reflects the success and popularity of the South Asian culture in the UK today. Many South Asians now within the western culture feel at home as they are able to watch Asian programmes on TV (star plus), watch Indian movies at the cinema and purchase Asian clothes, jewellery, food from places like Southall known as little India. Not just the South Asian community but you have people from 70 different nationalities and can embrace each of their culture in London.

Defining Stress

Individuals vary in the way in which they use the term 'stress' in their everyday language. The term 'stress' has been defined in several ways by psychologists differing in the emphasis of physiological, psychological factors, and the relationship between the individual and the environment (Ogden, 1996).

Biological Model

The most primitive model of stress was proposed by Cannon (1932), which was the 'flight and fight model' that is mainly physiological. The model suggests that external pressures elicit the flight or fight response, which increases the level of physiological arousal and activity rate to allow the individual to either dodge or fight the source of stress.

Another physiological model of stress is Selye's general adaptation syndrome (GAS) proposed in 1956. The model is based on the following three stages: (1) alarm stage which is when an individual increases in activity when exposed to a stressful event, (2) resistance which involves the individual trying to cope and undo the alarm stage, and (3) exhaustion which is when the individual fails to show any resistance when exposed to the stressor.

Psychological Model

Lazarus and Cohen (1973) developed a model of stress which considers the individual's psychological state. This model is more popularly known as 'the transactional model of stress'. According to Lazarus and Cohen (1973), individuals undergo two types of appraisals when they come across a stressful event: primary and secondary appraisal. Primary appraisal refers to evaluating the seriousness of an outcome such as its effect on the individual's well-being. Secondary appraisal refers to evaluating one's resources and options for coping with the demands. Thus stress takes place when we think that a specific event threatens our well-being because we do not have enough coping resources to deal with the event. Overall, the primary and secondary appraisals determine whether or not the individual views the subject matter stressful.

Social Model

Another perspective regarding the notion of stress was developed by Holmes and Rahe (1967), which was the life event theory. This theory looks at stress and stress-related changes as a response to life change. The theory includes a schedule of recent experiences (SRE), which is a list of life changes or events, which is presented to the respondents. These life changes/events vary from serious events such as death of a close member to moderate events such as pregnancy to minor events that include a change in eating or sleeping habits.

The scores are obtained by counting the number of actual recent experiences. Research indicates that the scores from the SRE reflect one's health status, e.g. the more stressful the life experience, the greater the likelihood it will affect one's health status.

This book uses the term 'stress' based on the popular notion of stress as described in the everyday lives of an individual and is based on what stress is according to the individual. The pressures resulting from stress can be *physical* (tension and high blood pressure), *psychological* (burnout and anxiety), or *social* (marital conflict and social isolation) to which individuals have to respond to (Baron, Byrne & Johnson, 1998). The definition of stress adapted in this research study is based on the respondent's interpretation of what stress is.

This research study is looking at the perceptions of stress as a response to life changes within an individual's life. Research indicates that events that involve strong demands tend to be stressful such as life transitions, i.e. changing from one phase to another in life (Moos and Schaefer, 1986). Some examples include the following: moving home, getting married, becoming a parent, losing a spouse through divorce, and migrating. The timing of a life transition can also affect the stress it produces. For example, if a life event is unexpected, then this can be considered stressful as one may be deprived of the resources to deal with the demands.

Cultural Impact of Stress

Looking at the research above, it would be interesting to see the cultural impact of stress as stress has a negative effect on both mental and physical health. It will be useful to examine some of the imminent forms of life transitions that are considered stressful. In relation to the role of culture on health, issues concerning 'migration' and 'culture clash' due to the differences within the individualistic and collectivist cultures are worth investigating.

Stress Sources Differ Across Culture

Individualistic cultures have self-originating stress whereas collectivist cultures have collectively originating stress. Collectivist individuals think of themselves as part of the community, and their goals and desires are the reflection of the community needs (Bhugra, 2004). Thus one can possibly assume that their stress is based on the needs of the family unit. Individualist and collectivist process stress differently. Certain stress sources such as financial or social/environment may vary. However, the major difference is that individuals within a collectivist culture feel that family is a major source of stress (Triandis, 1989).

As well as sources of stress, one may assume that coping strategies when dealing with stress cannot be generalised. Within individualistic cultures, individuals may seek physical exercise and create a positive effect by engaging in acts that create a positive effect. Collectivist cultures may seek social support from family and spirituality when dealing with stress.

Stress Can Lead to Illness

Stress has developed into an important characteristic of modern living, specifically because of the traditional family structures collapsing and the present-day urban environment. Individuals have a certain tolerance to stress, but when stress exceeds one's tolerance, it can lead to illness. There have been consistent findings proposing that acute and chronic stress is associated with down-regulation of the immune system (Marks, 2005). During everyday life, individuals come across several sources of stress such as problems in personal relationships (indifferent spouse/person) and environment disturbances (Baron et al., 1998). Such sources of stress can lead to anxiety and depression and may interfere with the individual's health-related behaviour, for instance poor diet, lack of exercise, and not getting enough sleep (Wibe & Mc Callium, 1986). This leads us to question the situations faced by those individuals who experience additional sources of stress apart from the everyday stressors.

Cultural Migration—an Under-researched Area

This research study is focusing on the South Asian population as there is less emphasis on collectivism as proposed by critical psychologists. One of the issues raised by critical psychologists is cultural migration. These individuals undergo additional sources of stress, which include the stress and strain of adjustments when moving to a new country, adapting to a new lifestyle, and the extent to which these individuals give value to their heritage culture in relation to the one they have migrated to. Also loss of familiar social networks and roles, language leading to communication difficulties, differences concerning the status of the older and younger people, and mental distress associated with adapting to different cultural values and customs (Maclachlan, 1997). Such distress may affect physical, psychological, and social aspects of health.

In relation to this, research has indicated that such emotional distress has led to depression and suicide in some cases amongst the migrated population (Burningham, 2001). Therefore, cultural adaptation may be associated with long-term health problems due to the 'culture clash' between the individualistic and collectivist cultures (Bhugra, 2004). Furthermore, there are several issues that have been raised by the South Asian communities themselves. Ram Gidoomal's (1993) book describes the Eastern and Western 'culture clash', showing Asians encountering difficulties living in an unfamiliar place. He talks about his family experience and the tragedy he faced such as differences in society norms, lifestyle, behaviour change, and attitudes. His book outlines the issues that majority of the South Asians faced when migrating to Britain and sketches some of the issues that are still tackled by South Asians today. These include feeling a sense of failure, poor self-esteem, and depressive symptoms, as many have problems with poor housing, unemployment, and 'culture clash' (Burningham, 2001).

In addition to these, migrants are also vulnerable to racism and discrimination. Not only is this another source of stress, but it is also a barrier to health promotion and personal development (e.g. access to health care, employment, benefits, and so forth) (Maclachan, 1997). Recently this has been highlighted through the reality programme 'Big Brother' in which an Asian celebrity living with three Caucasian individuals experienced bullying and racism due to the 'culture clash'. A reality programme like 'Big Brother' reflects some of the sources of stress Asian individual's face. This programme provoked 20,000 complaints to the TV regulators of channel 4. This led to a major controversy causing Gordon Brown, Tony Blair, and India's prime minister to get involved (Guardian, 2007). Being a celebrity and experiencing such behaviour can be dealt with, but what about those Asians who are not celebrities? There problems may be overlooked and they may suffer in silence.

My Critical Reflection

In conclusion, the major source of stress experienced by individuals within a collectivist culture is family attitudes, values, and beliefs (Anwar, 1998).

My aim is to provide research that could provide an outlook for others showing the additional sources of stress that Asian immigrants face. This will be done by providing an understanding of the challenges that can arise when living in two different worlds. This is similar to the conflict between Asian culture and the British culture that can be a source of anxiety for both South Asian parents migrated to Britain and their children who are either born or brought up in the Western nation.

Health care professionals need to be culturally sensitive to different ethnicities and trained on aspects of the South Asian culture. This will enable them to gain a better understanding of the South Asian individuals, appropriately targeting their needs, reducing stress levels, depression, and suicide rates (Maclachlan, 1997). My research study may also provide an opportunity for parents as well as their children to understand each other better, thus an effective measure to reduce stress and promote a healthy well-being.

CHAPTER 2

Research Study: The Perceptions of Stress amongst First and Second Generation South Asians in the UK

Aims of the Research

The aim of my research study is to look at the perceptions of stress in relation to family and lifestyle amongst South Asian parents living in England (first generation) who migrated from a collectivist culture in comparison with their children (second generation) who are born or brought up in England (individualistic culture) but have a collectivist background.

Rationale for the Chosen Population Asian Population

The perception of stress amongst the Caucasian population has been studied extensively. However studies targeting the perception of stress amongst individuals who have migrated into Britain is under researched. These individuals undergo additional sources of stress as there is a shift in their culture and identity. There is a dynamic and complex nature of issues associated with migration and the process of adapting to a different culture. This may often lead to psychological distress (Bhugra, 2004).

South Asian Population

The South Asian culture was chosen for this research study because they are the next largest population after Caucasians in England. Furthermore the South Asian population follow collectivist traditions whereas the Caucasian population follow individualistic traditions. Figure 1.1 below shows the distribution of ethnic group in England (*http://www.statistics.gov.uk/cci/nugget.asp?id=273*).

Population percetage in England

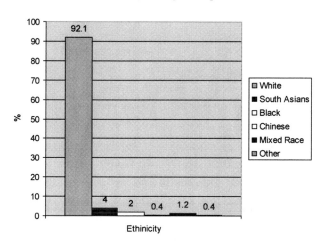

Westernised society and mainstream psychologists focus on individualism. The theoretical emphasis on psychology has been on Caucasian individuals, and studies on ethnic minorities such as South Asians within collectivist cultures have been rare (Maclachlan, 1997). This research study does not disregard the individualistic culture but to focus on the collectivist culture, as it is an under-researched area. Focusing on such research will help clinicians understand psychological distress experienced by individuals in the context of what is happening to them and their cultural changes in identity (Bhugra, 2004).

First and Second Generations

This research study looks at both the first and second generations, in order to capture the interpretation of both generations' accounts. This will enable both of the generations to gain an understanding of each other and come up with a solution, as the sources of stress that both generations face are intertwined with one another.

Research Objective

This research study can contribute to the role of health psychology in understanding the levels of stress associated with migration, which will facilitate the well-being of migrants as well as the receiving society, i.e. individualistic society in which the South Asians migrate. This will be achieved by producing cooperation to ensure a better understanding of cultures (Maclachlan, 1997).

Little attention has been given in examining the health status (well-being), beliefs, and perceptions of the different types of stress that migrated individuals may undergo. This research study also aims to fill in the gap within the literature, as critical psychologists propose that cultural migration is an under-researched area (Maclachlan, 1997).

The purpose of this research study is to firstly promote health by finding a balance between the individualistic and collectivist cultures for a healthy well-being for both parents and their children. Individuals from a collectivist culture may experience restrictions on personal freedom and demands of personal sacrifice. Thus they may need some aspects of individualistic entities such as autonomy. Some may take advantage of the individualistic entities, thus being selfish as a sense of community is eroded, leaving them being isolated (Maclachan, 1997).

Furthermore, research indicates that too much individualism may lead to social pathology such as crime, divorce, and child abuse (Bhugra, 2004). We need to promote being independent without wearing away a sense of community. We need to provide the same sort of health services as mainstream psychologists but consider cultural factors. This is because it is impossible to impose Western psychology on non-Western problems. Give people the strength of the collective identity but not at the price of having to disregard one's universal rights to health and welfare (Maclachlan, 1997).

Finding the middle ground and keeping a balance is easier said than done, which is why it may be worth offering research to help in the successful living of both parents and their children. By showing both the generations and helping them understand the needs of each other and the need for their own space is important. Being born in India and brought up in England in both the Eastern and Western cultures, I understand the psychological issues that can and do arise for both the younger and older generations. The younger generation should learn to value their Eastern culture. The older generation should be encouraged to learn and value the Western culture, creating a necessary balance for healthier relationships, better understanding, and a much more optimistic mental attitude (Ranu, 2007).

In today's society, some of the younger South Asians are facing difficulties and challenges by trying to keep a balance between their family values of Eastern culture, rules, and expectations, and the Western culture in which they are born into. This does not, however, mean that the young South Asian generations do not value their roots and parental upbringing; it just means that both generations need to have a compromise and balance to enable them all to live life together in harmony (Ranu, 2007).

This book aims to help South Asian families overcome the barriers, difficulties which their practising culture, families, society, religion, and beliefs bring into their lives. This will help enhance the understanding addressed to the South Asian society between the two generations due to the 'culture clash' they face. The South Asian society has a long way to go before they fully understand the Eastern and Western cultures. This is so because since the South Asian and ethnic society is formed by many mainstream religions, beliefs, and systems from around the world, it would be impossible for them all to understand the psychological effects on the two cultures (Ranu, 2007). However, we need to start somewhere. This book will be an excellent reading on this subject because this is a subject that once delved into will only keep on growing and extending. This book deals with opposing views that include taboo versus tradition and orthodox values versus progressive values, which are always entitled to a discussion.

Method

Participants

The sample number of participants that were used in this research study was a total of sixteen, with seven participants from the first generation and nine participants from the second generation. The participants from the first generation were recruited from the South Asian society. This is a registered charity that aims to improve the conditions of life of South Asians in Devon and Cornwall who are in need of social welfare, occupation due to their financial hardship or social circumstances. The South Asian society also promotes racial harmony and encourages better understanding of social, religious, and other needs of the community *(http://www.southasiansociety.co.uk/)*.

Participants from the second generation were recruited from hi5 and Facebook, which are online global networks for young individuals. These networks enable young individuals to open up their own personal page, create and explore content, and voice their opinions on discussion forums and message boards (*http://www.hi5networks.com/aboutus.html, http://www. facebook.com/about.php*).

Details for the selection process are presented in Appendix I. Due to a great number of responses; participant accounts were randomly selected on the basis of detail rather than closed answers. Also after achieving the target sample number, I stopped with the collection of data for this research study. However, individuals were still given the opportunity to continue with filling in the online survey if they wish to.

Material

An online survey on the Internet was used to gather the participants' insight about the issues based on the notions of stress amongst first- and second-generation South Asians in the context of cultural migration and family dynamics. The online survey included a different set of questions for both the first- and second-generation participants (see Appendix II). The web site also included a consent form with instructions. This consent form included what is required from them, and participants were informed that their identity would not be physically attached to the final data produced (see Appendix III). At the end of the study, participants received an online debriefing, which included the aims of the study and also contact details (see Appendix IV).

Ethical Issues

Before the study started, participants were informed on the online survey home page about the nature of the study and the participants' rights of participating in the study. Consent of the participant was achieved before they took part in the online survey. Participants were told that all the information they submit will remain anonymous and confidential, and if they choose to withdraw, they are free to do so at any time.

The study did not expect to involve any risk of discomfort or harm, but in the event of this, participants were given full debriefing, explaining the aims of the study along with contact details. Also participants were given the opportunity to ask questions or raise any concerns.

Procedure

Participants were asked to click on to the online web site given to them to take part in the study (www.staff.city.ac.uk/psychstudies/sb/). The online web site appeared with background information regarding this research study allowing participants to decide whether or not they would like to take part in the study. If participants agreed to take part, they were asked to click on to the 'start survey' icon. A consent form then appeared, asking the participants to tick the box so that they agree to take part. A set of instructions then appeared, telling the participants what to do, which was to click on to the age group that best describes them, and fill in the demographic information. After completion of the demographic detail, an open-ended survey appeared to seek insight and meaning about the participants' experience (see Appendix V). In the consent form, the participants were encouraged to elaborate on particular issues by asking for in-depth answers. This enabled me to gain an extended account of my participants' lived/current experience. Thus both participants from the first and second generations were asked to talk about their experiences regarding their perceptions of stress. Questions were asked to seek insight into the participants' experience, perceptions, feelings, and life events. The results for both the target groups (first and second generations) were accessed via their own web sites (*www.staff.city.ac.uk/psychstudies/sb/ Secure/Gen1.txt* and www.staff.city.ac.uk/psychstudies/sb/Secure/Gen2.txt). To view the results in a systematic manner, the results for both target groups were saved in Edexcel.

Rationale for Chosen Methodology

The Internet is a new method of data collection that can provide researchers the opportunity to access written material signifying our worlds and people's desires, concerns, and thoughts. This type of research prevents methodological issues such as recruiting participants. This is because individuals do not have to be physically present at a specific time and location to participate in the study. This finding corresponds with White and Dorman (2000), who used a similar method of collection that includes online support groups. As the online survey was available on the Internet, it gave me the ability to access a great deal of accounts, as this method of data collection wipes away the restrictions posed on the participants of time and location (Eysenbach & Till, 2001).

Furthermore, the present study used online discussion board groups that were generated on hi5 and Facebook to access respondents from the second generation. This is because the Internet is a popular medium amongst the young generation, specifically global networks such as hi5 and Facebook. The Internet also enabled participants to present their account anonymously without revealing their identity and the opportunity to decide what information they wanted to disclose over the Internet. Furthermore, for this reason, the survey used in the study was made online as this gave the participants the opportunity to disclose their thoughts and feeling without any restrictions, as the accounts were made anonymous so the participants can talk about more sensitive issues that they may not be able to at face value (Eysenbach & Till, 2001). This is further supported by Coulson (2005), who used online social support networks as a method of data collection.

Keeping the participants' accounts anonymous meant that the participants' personal identity was not physically attached to the data produced, which could not be accessed by other participants as well as myself. Nevertheless, ethical issues in qualitative research were considered, as Internet research raises new issues in research ethics. As the Internet is a global network which is a public domain, using such a method for data collection can also affect the study of research (Eysenbach & Till, 2001). Sometimes the participants may not be willing to participate, as their accounts are posted on the Internet which is made publicly visible. Thus the present study took perceived privacy, informed consent, and potential harm into consideration (Eysenbach & Till, 2001). Participants were made aware that any information they disclose will remain confidential and anonymous. Consent was obtained to allow participants to further participate in the study, and finally in the event of discomfort, a debriefing page and contact details were provided.

Furthermore, the online survey included open-ended questions acquiring depth. The questions presented to the participants were concerning general ideas and issues so that the participants can elaborate on them. The respondents were given a chance to talk about their stories, as I was relying on respondents to identify and explain what was important to them. Thus the process was non-directive and not bias in any way (Murray & Chamberlain, 1999). Ethical approval from a formal committee other than City University was not needed for this particular research.

Analysis and Discussion

The written accounts were analysed using thematic analysis. Thematic analysis is used for identifying, analysing, and reporting patterns (themes) within qualitative data. This type of analysis allows flexibility to report and explore the experiences, meanings, and the reality of the participants in rich detail. Furthermore, the analysis can also be used to recognise the ways in which individuals make sense of their experiences and consequently how the larger social context influences on these meanings (Braun & Clarke, 2006). (Please see Appendix VI for details on the stages of thematic analysis and the author's methodological reflection on the process.)

All the responses and individual analysis are presented in Appendices VII and VIII. The respondent number and the location of the quotes will be illustrated as shown below throughout the text, e.g. respondent 1, lines 2-6 as [1:2-6]. In the next section, I will present themes from the first and second generations' online survey. The role of culture amongst the first and second generation South Asians in England was investigated. First generation refer to those who have migrated from a collectivist culture whereas the second generation refer to those who were born or brought up in England. The themes that have emerged from the online surveys include the following:

- Changes encountered during migration
- First and second generations' sources of stress
- Culture clash
- Generation gap
- Family dynamics
- Psychological well-being
- Coping methods (for clustered themes, see Appendix IX)

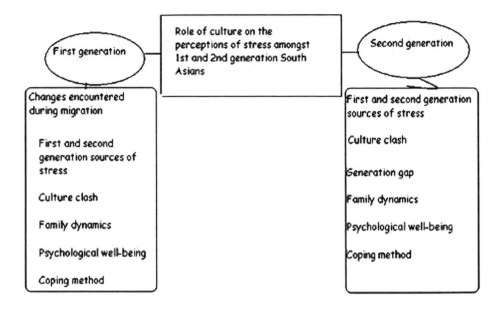

Fig. 1. First- and second-generation themes

Themes from the First Generation

Changes Encountered during Migration

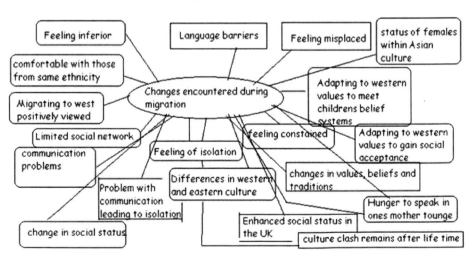

**Fig. 2. Some of the codes emerged from theme
(changes encountered during migration)**

One of the themes that emerged from the online surveys is 'changes encountered during migration'. When migrating to a country that is different from one's heritage, an individual undergoes several changes that include adapting to a new culture and lifestyle (Maclachlan, 1997). Respondents expressed that they experienced a loss in social network when migrating in England because of limited social support (see *[1:2-6]*, *[2:8-9]*, and *[7:9-10]*). They found generating a social network within the UK difficult compared to their heritage culture.

'when I migrated to UK in 2005, had to seek out the south Asian families living in my immediate milieu and make attempts to make meaningful new friendships with families we could vibe with, so as to provide a new avenue for all my family members to socialize with other south Asians [6:4-7].

First generation's social network in the UK comprised of a few South Asians from the South Asian society who had also migrated from back home. They felt more comfortable and better understood with individuals from the same ethnicity (see *[1:6-8]*, *[3:12-14]*, *[3:37-38]*, and *[5:12-14]*). However, after living in England for some time, the respondents made progress in widening their social network by interacting with those from different ethnicities through work (see *[3:14-15]*). Along with social network, South Asians experienced a change in social status. Respondents expressed that their social status enhanced as migrating to the West is positively viewed with improving one's socio-economic status back home (see *[1:8-9]* and *[1:9-12]*).

South Asian females also experienced a change in role from a housewife to a working woman. Females found it difficult working in England due to two main reasons: (1) being an Asian woman and (2) working in a predominantly Caucasian society (see *[2:9-12]*). Within the Asian culture, females were often seen ready for marriage after education. However, when migrating to the West, South Asian females came across equal opportunities where men are not the only breadwinners.

My social status has changed. In India after my education . . . I got married . . . as after education that is what happens within Asian families . . . I came to this country where I was a house wife which was expected as this what happens within the Asian culture but . . . started to work which is different to what is expected within the Asian culture' [3:15-18] and *[7:12-14].*

South Asians have also adapted to the Western values and beliefs to make themselves more acceptable to others, hence enhancing their social circle (see *[2:13-14]* and *[7:10-12]*). The first generation has adapted to the Western values of equal opportunities and being broad minded for a healthy upbringing for their children. This has enabled young South Asians to discuss matters more openly, which are taboo within the Asian culture (see *[3:24-26]*). Also this has given South Asians the opportunity to question the collectivist values regarding personal sacrifice for the need of others (Schoeneman, 1997). Respondents suggested that self-satisfaction is sometimes more important than sacrificing one's goal for the benefit of one's family (see *[5:27-29]*).

South Asians have also readjusted their values and customs due to the difference in cultural and social environment (see *[6:16-17]*). The difference in culture (see *[6:18-21]*) has led South Asians experiencing low self-esteem since the rules that they have learnt for certain subject matters such as friendship and humour do not apply within the Western culture (see *[2:34-35]*).

In addition, South Asians encountered communication problems due to the language barriers they experienced when migrating. Respondents could not speak fluent English or understand the British sense of humour and vice versa. Respondents expressed that Caucasian individuals used slang with regional dialects, which made it difficult for them to understand (see *[2:17-22]*). Problems in communication further led respondents feeling afraid to speak up in public, consequently feeling socially isolated.

Communication in the beginning was next to zero . . . I pronounced it wrong and the class would make fun of me [5:34-38]) (see *[7:14-15]* and *[3:15-18]*). This finding coincides with Burningham (2001), who suggested that having difficulty with the English language can be a precursor of stress, which can lead to the feeling of isolation due to communication difficulties. Language barriers also led South Asians longing to speak in their mother tongue *[see 6:11-13]*. Nevertheless, respondent's mention that now they are able to understand and communicate in English by interacting through work (see *[3:22-24]*), and through the participating in English-learning classes. This was perceived as some of the tools in helping them to understand and communicate in English (see *[5:14-15]*).

Furthermore, migrating in England has led South Asians feeling inferior (*the early years were not easy as being different in the country can lead to a kind of inferiority* complex stress [2:36-38]), constrained (*no friends, felt alone as I was home bound [4:8-9]*), misplaced (*when I came to England . . . felt isolated and lost . . . massive change . . . in terms of culture and tradition [3:10-1]*), and isolated (*felt a stranger amongst the majority white population . . . of immigrants [6:8-9]*). South Asians have experienced problems in setting up a new existence in an unfamiliar place without any social support, experiencing communication difficulties (see [5:11-12]) and loss of familiar networks (see [3:30-33] and [5:53-55]).

South Asians also experienced discrimination (Maclachan, 1997) (*had to stand for hours . . . was taken for granted as I was new and didn't speak much of English . . . did not know how to speak English my colleagues would laugh at me because of my accent, thus I faced discrimination . . . isolated [3:33-36]*). This can be distressing when adapting to different cultural values and customs (Maclachan, 1997).

Overall, first-generation respondents proposed that 'culture clash' still remains even after some people living in England for some time (see [1:1-2]). Although they are now learning through their children to adapt to more of the Western values (see [2:22-25]), they remain to abide by the South Asian cultural values (*still religious and spiritual . . . changed some aspects of myself in terms of what I wear which is western clothes . . . not smoking, being in a relationship, having a good education and respecting elders [7:18-21]*).

First and Second Generations' Sources of Stress

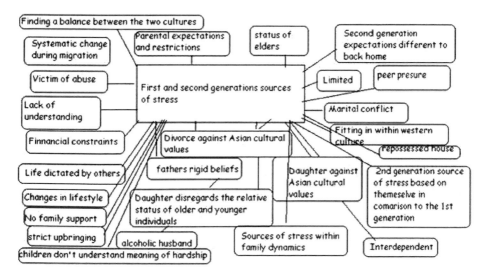

**Fig. 3. Some codes emerged from the theme
(First and second generations' sources of stress)**

Another theme that emerged is first and second generations' sources of stress. The systematic change during migration was the primary source of stress for the first generation, as they had to build their existence (*stress was largely associated with systematic change . . . language (pronunciations), behavioural differences . . . financial constraints and the need to face and satisfy the expectations of back home was also an elements of stress to me [1:18-22]*).

This was especially hard for those females who had migrated alone to the West, as they became the primary carer having their families dependent on them ([see *6:32-36]*).

In addition, migration had led to a change in lifestyle that was different from their own heritage culture (*with no cook, domestic servant available running a family becomes very challenging and stressful especially for a full time job and career aspirations [6:37-39]*). First generation experienced stressful challenges in bringing up their children within the Western culture (*my younger child is a stress for me as she is very much influenced by the western values of doing what she wants to and is exposed to several western values which go against the Asian tradition . . . voice [3:51-54]*). This is supported by Ghuman (1999), who accounts where South Asians want their children to abide by some of the collectivist values, as they are much influenced by the Western values (see *[3:47]*) and hence find it hard balancing between the two differing cultures.

'Main stress as a Asian father is because we are living in an environment where the children are facing two different cultures . . . big challenge to teach your children what they should do and what they shouldn't [3:59-62].

Furthermore, as *inter*dependence is emphasised within the South Asian culture, South Asians constantly worry about settling their children with a secure future (see *[3:48-49]*). Hence stress is based on the needs of the family unit (Triandis, 1989). Respondents expressed that young South Asians experience too much individualism hence engage in inappropriate behaviour that conflicts with collectivist values (*daughter left education . . . became involved into the western culture of smoking, going around with boys, wearing in appropriate clothing. She argues with me and doesn't treat me as her mum but someone her age that she can shout at rather than respect [7:46-50]*). This is supported by Bhugra (2004), who mentions that too much individualism can lead to social pathology.

Furthermore, South Asians propose that their children do not understand them, as the restrictions they pose on their children are for their own benefit (*they think that their parents are their enemies but do not realize that it is only for their own good . . . becoming pregnant at an early age [7:54-59]*). Also respondents believe that the second generation does not understand the seriousness of the sources of stress that their parents have encountered (*elements of my stress are laughable for the . . . second generation migrants [1:23-24]*).

Nevertheless, the first generation acknowledge the second generation's source of stress which is associated with forced marriages, mixed expectations due to 'culture clash', emphasis on the importance of education, strict restrictions, and discrimination (see *[1:24-25]*, *[1:25-28]*, *[3:54-57]*, and *[4:47-50]*). The first generation places strict expectations on their children with regards to the importance of education due to the hardship that they have experienced (see *[7:29-33]*).

Respondents acknowledged that the second generation may find 'fitting in' within the Western culture as a challenge (*second generation has to deal with added stressor called as peer pressure. They get caught between the cultural differences of the eastern and western cultures [6:39-41]*). However, they suggest that the second generation should not act repulsively against their Asian value system despite no longer being influenced by their social network back home (*However as a first generation migrant, I was not revolting against my value system . . . well behaved child to my parents [1:28-30]*).

Furthermore, respondents propose that the second generation's sources of stress are based on themselves whereas their stress comprises themselves and others within their personal system (*my stress is based on my children whereas their stress is based on themselves [7:53-54]*).

First-generation South Asians suggest that the second generation become stressed over minor events (see *[6:41]*) and are unaware of what hardship is [*learn the English culture . . . build everything from scratch and learnt most of the things hard way . . . children take things for granted because things are already there for them . . . more less for them comparing to what we had [5:67-70]).* They also believe that the second generation does not understand the value of money, as they have not experienced financial hardship (see *[5:73-75]*).

Nevertheless, respondents mention that some of their past sources of stress are caused by their rigid Asian cultural values that they were brought up with. This includes strict upbringing where South Asians are taught to abide by their parents' strict restrictions and expectations despite what they believe (Anwar, 1998) (*I was brought up in a very strict environment . . . not allowed to go to any social events with the friends. Father used to dictate the way we were living . . . conversation [5:38-42] and got married there were a lot of things that I wanted to experience but never had chance in the past [5:55-58]).* It also includes the status of the elders where individuals need to be respectful and obedient towards the decisions made by those who are elder despite their beliefs (Schoeneman, 1997) (*As he was the head of the house others views within the family were not taken into consideration [2:41-42]).* This is further supported by South Asian females proposing that their husbands were unable to provide any support when they became victims of abuse in the past since South Asians were brought up to simply abide by their elders.

'Was abused from my father in law as I could not do what I would want. I wasn't allowed to talk to my parents . . . from back home and they were sometimes told that I wasn't at home even though I was. I was a victim of abuse. I was put under restrictions and felt suffocated. Although my husband had little say because of his father' [3:42-46]. This finding corresponds with Schoeneman (1997), who proposed that individuals within a collectivist culture have less control and limited freedom (Maclachan, 1997).

Furthermore, the relative status of males and females within the Asian culture was also a source of stress for South Asian females, as males were given more importance than females (*my family also did not have enough money to educate us all . . . within the family [4:17-18]).* Due to male dominance, females were unable to act in accordance with their will, hence experienced marital conflict (*my husband in the UK wanted me to cut ties with my family so I got separated after a lot of struggle [4:37-38]*) and felt limited (*My uncle treated me bad and abused me he put several restrictions on me on what I could do and could not do [4:39-40]*) since their life was being dictated by others (*restricted to go out with friends being an adult and do not have my own life as it is dictated by others [4:44-45]).*

This has further led some South Asian women to go through divorce, hence going against Asian cultural values (Anwar, 1998) (*I went through a divorce at a young age . . . difficult as within the Asian culture it is seen shameful . . . many fingers pointed at from Asian family and friends [4:40-43]*). Research further indicates that such distress has led Asian women experiencing stress and depression (Burningham, 2001). Another source of stress for the South Asian population involves the pressure to satisfy the strict family expectations that their 'shame-based' culture puts on them (Anwar, 1998). This is reflected within the first generation's account (*the need to face and satisfy the expectations from back home . . . was stress to me [1:22-23]*). Since migrating to the West is assumed to enhance one's socio-economic status, South Asian families are expected to send money back home to support their families (*I started working as a domestic cleaner and sent the money I had back home to support my brothers [7:38-39]*).

Overall, the first generation's major sources of stress were family attitudes, values, and beliefs (Anwar, 1998). The complex issues associated with migration and adapting to a new culture have also led the first generation experiencing psychological distress (Bhugra, 2004).

Culture Clash

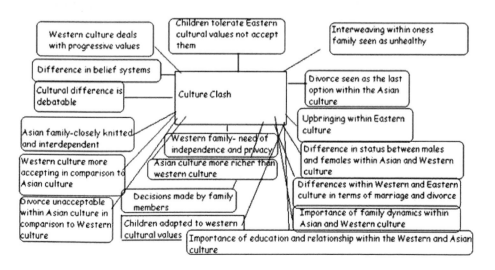

Fig. 4. Some codes emerged from theme (culture clash)

The psychological distress the first generation experience is due to 'culture clash'. Culture clash refers to the differences between Asian and Western cultures. For example, the Asian culture emphasises the importance of family dynamics (Ghuman 1999). This puts tremendous responsibility and expectations on South Asians, as they have been brought up to be *inter*dependent and value the importance of the caring for others (*was brought up the all of us way, puts a lot of responsibility . . . expectations on you . . . try to please your family and extended family [2:44-46]*).

Since Asian families emphasise the importance of togetherness, decisions are made by those that are elder, regardless of what age group you belong to (see *[3:3-5]*). Whereas the Western culture traditionally emphasises independence and privacy. Individuals do not live with their extended family, which allows them the freedom to make their own decisions [see *[3:5-7]*). It was perceived that the Western culture views interweaving and socialising too much within the family as unhealthy (see *[2:4-5]*). However, family is of importance within the West, but there is a clear distinction between independence and *inter*dependence whereas within the Asian culture these boundaries are not clear cut (see *[2:2-4]*).

The relative status of males and females also differs between the two cultures. Within the Asian culture, females are expected to be reserved, study only to a certain degree and then get married. By contrast, males are encouraged to voice their opinion and to study further as this is 'bringing honour and glory to the family' (Ghuman, 1999) since they are taking on board the family name (see *[3:7-9]*). Western cultures on the other hand are encouraged to value gender equality (Schoeneman, 1997).

Furthermore, certain subject matters are regarded as taboo within the Asian culture whereas the Western culture is seen as more accepting. Divorce is looked down upon within the Asian culture (Ghuman 1991), hence South Asian females are more likely to accommodate an unsuccessful marriage in comparison with their Caucasian counterparts (*divorce is seen as taboo my father knew that no one would marry me in India so he got me married to someone abroad . . . Hindu [7:33-36]*) (see *[2:6-8]*).

Intimacy is also viewed differently within the East and West. Within the Western culture, it is acceptable for individuals to fall in love, move in together before marriage, and get divorced if there is no marital satisfaction (Dion et al., 1993). However within the Asian culture, this is frowned upon (see *[5:6-10]*). Overall, premarital sex, dating, and divorce are forbidden within the Asian culture in comparison with the Western culture (Delphy et al., 1992) (see *[3:26-30]*). Furthermore, education and the respect of elders are emphasised within the Asian culture (see *[1:15-18]* and *[7:3-5]*).

In addition, Asian culture values the importance of *inter*dependence (*Asian families are more bonded together [5:5]*) whereas the Western culture emphasises independence (*most cases children, after the age of 16, like to live independently [5:4]*). The Asian culture deals with preserving traditions whereas the Western culture deals with progressive values (see *[2:1-2]*). Hence the Western culture is perceived as more accepting than the Asian culture (*everything is openly accepted within western culture whereas there are . . . restrictions within the Asian culture . . . within western culture [4:4-8]*).

'Culture clash' is also causing challenges for South Asian parents when bringing up their children. The conflict arises due to the difference in belief systems between the first and second generations (*the biggest difference between the two cultures in my personal experience is my culture was and is still very much based on all of us, whilst my children's belief systems are based on me, me, me [2:28-30]*) (see *[2:40-4]*). This is further supported by the first generation still abiding by the traditional Asian cultural values whereas the second generation wanting to move on with progressive vales (see *[1:28-30]*).

Respondents suggest that the second generation try to tolerate the Asian values but not accept them (*my children first and far most British . . . they tolerate my old customs . . . make it clear that they do not necessarily believe in them [1:25]*). Overall, the conflict is arising due to the beliefs, values, and traditions, which shape one's family dynamic (Ghuman 1999).

Nevertheless, first-generation respondents propose that the second generation is not at fault in dismissing the eastern values, as they are brought up as independent thinkers within the Western world (see *[2:27-28]*).

Family Dynamics

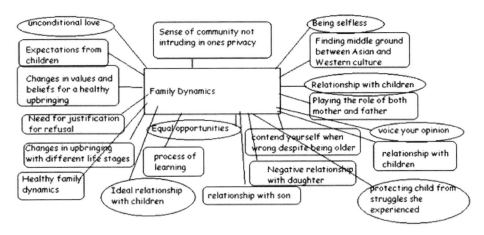

Fig. 5. Some codes emerged from theme (family dynamics)

The impact of the Western culture has led traditional Asian family dynamics collapsing (Baron, 1998) but not necessarily for the worst. The change in traditional family dynamics has led South Asians in the UK to embrace the importance of equality (*every member of the family is treated equal* and *There is no difference in husband and wife when it comes to doing everyday jobs in the house . . . should be equal rights* (see *[5:76-77]* and *[79-82]*), justification for refusal rather than imposing one's views (*did not have any guts to question him . . . should have justification for saying no and make sure that the children do not interoperate that in different way* and *have to say no to them for anything, you should have some valid reason and you should explain to the children why you said no [5:63-66]* and *[92-94]*), understanding the need for changes in upbringing in accordance with different life stages (see *[5:88-92]*), voicing one's opinions rather than suffering in silence (*If you are right in whatever you are doing never be intimidated by anyone. Do not be afraid to form your opinion [5:95-96]*), and having the ability to contend oneself when wrong despite being older (*if you are ever wrong then do not argue. Don't be ashamed to apologies to person even if that person is younger than you. Do not have ego inside you [5:97-98]*).

The traditional Asian family structures are also changing from nuclear families to the acceptance of lone parents due to unfortunate circumstances, specifically for females (see *[4:54-56]*). Furthermore, a change in traditional family dynamics is leading to healthy relationships between parents and children (see *[4:54]* and *[6:44-46]*) since parents are adjusting to the Western culture for their children (*became open minded for my children and understanding . . . differences within the culture and did not want my children to face the difficulties as I did [4:24-26]*) and finding the middle ground between the Asian and Western cultures (see *[4:27-30]*). Hence some parents are expanding their collectivist value systems (Weinreich, 1996) and absorbing some Western values. They are beginning to see some aspects of the Western culture as a source of learning rather than discarding it completely but at the same time maintaining the values from their heritage culture (Orozco &-Orozco, 2001).

Nevertheless, respondents suggest that sometimes their children's perceptions does not meet with theirs as they are impatient (see *[4:52-54]* and *[56-58]* and *[3:67-69]*). Hence some South Asians experience a negative relationship with their children (*My eldest daughter is very disruptive and has no respect for me . . . not wrong [7:64-66]*). The respondents also proposed that the second generation is not always at fault, as the parents put pressure on their children by having too many expectations (*feel sometimes that I expect a lot from them—in terms of grades at school, what chores they should do at home, how much time they should spend with their grandparents [2:57-59]*). Such strict expectations may lead young South Asians experiencing psychological distress (Anwar, 1998). Nonetheless, the respondents mention that the expectations that they place on their children are to protect their children from the struggles that they have experienced (see *[7:64-65]*).

In addition, some South Asians who are within the traditional family system perceive an ideal family as comprising a sense of community without intruding one's privacy (*an ideal family is close but not in each other's pocket [2:49]*), being selfless rather than selfish (*they are there for each other in times of happiness and sadness but should not put too many expectations of each other because . . . disappointment tends to follow, with worse [2:49-52]*), sharing unconditional love (*An ideal family should have unconditional love for each other, with the proviso 'this is who and what I am—accept me as I am—and love me as I am [2:52-53]*), and better understanding between parent and child (*my children having an understanding of their parents not arguing with their parents and respect . . . share their problems with me [3:57-58]*).

Overall, the first generation seek for healthy family dynamics that consists of a *Good husband, children who have an understanding. A family that understands each other and su ports each other through thick and thin. There's love trust and mainly a great understanding [7:59-62].* Respondents acknowledge this as a learning process and can be achieved with time (see *[5:98-100]*). As finding a balance between the Asian and Western cultures is a challenge itself as too much collectivism can lead to sacrificing one's freedom (Maclachan, 1997) and too much individualism can lead to social pathology (Bhugra, 2004).

Psychological Well-being

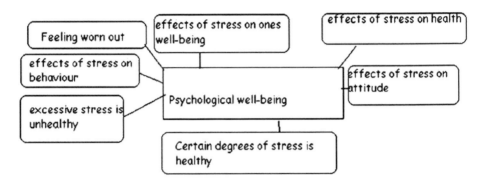

Fig. 6. Some codes emerged from theme (psychological well-being)

Another theme that emerged from the respondents' accounts is psychological well-being. Stress has both positive and negative effects on one's physical and mental well-being. Certain degree of stress is positively viewed and seen as healthy (*Small stress is good for our brain because it stimulates the brain to carry out the activities [5:1-2]*). Respondents suggest that stress is an essential part of living, as it brings out a challenge (see *[6:47-49]*). Nevertheless excessive stress can be unhealthy (*too much stress can be bad for health [5:2]*).

Furthermore, stress can have a negative effect on one's attitude (*I start to hate my life and feel that I want to commit suicide but then I think about my children. my attitude is negative [7:67-69]* and *have a negative attitude I am quiet impulsive and see everyone and everything in the wrong way as I have trouble with viewing what is right and wrong [3:70-72]*). Stress also has a negative effect on one's behaviour (*I want to be alone; I feel angry, sad, low and want to leave everyone and everything and go away [3:69-70], cannot eat and cry a lot [7:66-67],* and *I can think straight, I want to cry and want to be left alone [4:58-50]*).

The first-generation respondents suggest that stress has a negative effect on their mental and physical health. Listed below are a few examples:

- *Feeling . . . tired and exhausted [1:1]*
- *Sleep gets affected and I become tired I get headaches and take many paracetamol [4:59-60]*
- *I have suffered from stress in the last few years . . . this has in turn made me suffer from IBS—a digestive health problem that has resulted directly from years of stress. I also get stomach ulcers from time to time [2:63-66]*
- *Had stroke . . . now [:108-110]* and *went through depression earlier when I suffered through stress [7:68-69].* This is further supported by Baron (1998)

Coping Method

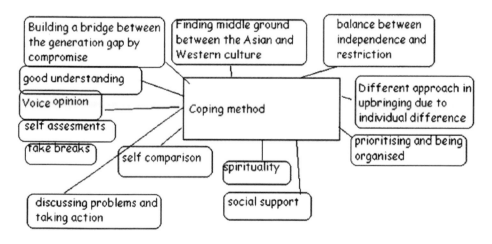

Fig. 7. Some codes emerged from theme (coping method)

Coping method was the final theme that emerged from the first generation's accounts. The theme is divided into two sub-headings: (1) coping strategies that the respondents use to deal with stress in general and (2) coping strategies used to cope with stress within the family.

The coping strategies that respondents use when generally stressed included a change in focus (see *[1:37-38]*), discussing the problems and taking action (see *[2:68-73]*), social support (see *[4:60-61]* and *[5:77-79]*), self-assessment *[6:50-53]*, self-comparison *[2:38-39]*, being organised (see *[5:110-113]*, and spirituality (see *[7:70-71]*).

To reduce the psychological conflict within one's family dynamics, respondents propose individuals to voice their opinions *[5:82]*, parents and children to build a bridge between the generation gap (see *[2:41-44]* and *[59-60]*), use a different approach in upbringing, considering individual differences *[5:102-104]*, parents finding a balance between independence and restriction with regards to their children (see *[5:86-88]*), and finally both parents and children finding the middle ground between the Asian and Western cultures *[4:27-30]*. This is further supported by Ranu (2007), who proposes a need for a balance between the Asian and Western cultures in order to reduce psychological conflict. Overall, a good understanding is needed within one's family dynamics to reduce psychological distress *[5:83-85]*.

Themes from the Second Generation

First and Second Generations' Sources of Stress

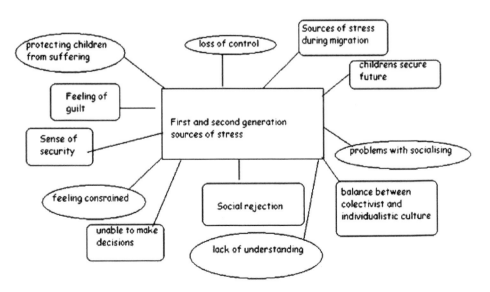

Fig. 8. Some of the codes emerged from theme (first and second generations' sources of stress)

Similar to the first generation, one of the main themes that has emerged in the second generation's accounts is first and second generations' sources of stress. The second generation's major source of stress results from the difference in perceptions and beliefs between their parents and themselves.

Respondents propose that they have a lack of control when making decisions, as the control lies within their parents' judgements of right from wrong; despite being adults themselves (*I am not allowed to go out a lot . . . not fair when you are 22 you are classified as an adult [6:10-11]* and (see *[6:35-36]*)).

This is further supported by Schoeneman (1997), who suggested that collectivists have no control, as this belongs to the personal system to which they belong to. Respondents hence feel frustrated, as they believe that they are old enough thus capable of making their own decisions. In addition, the second generation experience difficulties with socialising due to the restrictions put forward by their parents (*want to go out with friends it is always an issue . . . parents know who I am going with . . . still it's a problem [4:15-17]* and (see *[3:15]*)). The problem in socialising is a result of 'culture clash', as within a collectivist culture socialising largely comprises immediate and extended family. Hence young South Asians are finding it hard to understand and deal with the demands of both the individualistic and collectivist cultures (Ghuman, 1991).

Another form of stress that the respondents outline is parental pressure. Respondents suggest that their parents pressurise them to do well in education, as they want their children to have a secure future (*pushed to find a job and support and save financially [3:30]*). Respondents acknowledge the reason why parents pressurise them to get a job and good grades and save financially, as they do not want their children to suffer like they did when migrating in England (*lack of education has led them urging their children to perform well . . . with no education establishing a well-paid job has also been difficult for them [3:5-7]*). Furthermore, the second generation acknowledge that their parents worry about their secure future and provide support (*parent's main biggest stress is settling their children and getting a good education. Until the children get a good job and start earning the parents will always be stressed [4:45-47]*).

However, due to the strict expectations, young South Asians feel that their ambitions are not theirs but their parents (*perform for them rather than myself [3:37-38]*) thus feel guilty if they fail to achieve them (see *[3:28-29]*). This finding corresponds with Radhakrishna and Chan (1997), where individuals within a collectivist culture give the same importance to their parents and their ambitions. This signifies a true reflection of the collectivist culture of what one wants to do needs to be approved by family since the collectivist culture is based on those around you not oneself. Such restrictions and expectations have left young South Asians feeling constrained and unable to voice their opinion *[see 2:14 and 23]*.

Nevertheless, respondents recognise the current and past first generations' sources of stress such as adapting to different lifestyle and culture relative to the one that they have migrated from (see *[3:1-4]*) and now saving financially for their children's secure future until their children are settled (see *[5:24-30]*). This is because individuals within a collectivist culture are brought up to make personal sacrifices for their families (Shaw, 1988). Overall, the second generation's source of stress results from family dynamics, which is due to the lack of understanding between the parent and children (*I don't understand my parents, she doesn't understand that everyone is different, and I've explained . . . not listen [4:16, 28, and 41-42]*). This in turn seems to be the basis of not only the second generation's but also the first generation's sources of stress. This corresponds with Anwars's (1998) finding.

'Social rejection' is also a source of stress for the second generation. This is due to the difference in upbringing within the Western and Asian cultures, perhaps further leading young South Asians to adapt to some of the Western values (*I have also in the past faced discrimination . . . because of my background or how I have been brought up [3:33-35]* and reject the Asian values to fit in with society.

This further supports the clash in the first and second generations' thoughts due to the 'culture clash'. Within the Asian culture, South Asians are not allowed to date before they establish a secure future (see *[3:32-33]*) and have to marry someone who can uphold the traditions (see *[2:15-16]*). However, within the Western culture, dating is natural during adolescence.

Therefore, young South Asians find it hard maintaining a balance between the Western culture they are exposed to and the Eastern culture proposed by their families (see *[2:5-6]*).

In addition, Ghuman (1991) proposes that living between two different cultures is a demanding experience where several conflicts arise. Thus the clash in views mirrors the 'culture clash' between the distinct Eastern and Western believes and value system. The online survey further supports Ghuman's finding that young South Asians want fewer restrictions and want their lifestyle not a bad name to shame their parents. They do not agree with some of the collectivist values due to what they perceive around them within the Western culture.

Culture Clash

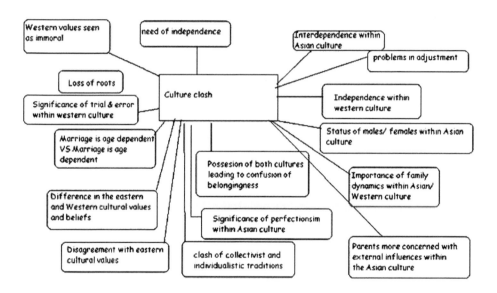

Fig. 9. Some codes emerged from theme (culture clash)

Respondents acknowledge the differences between the Asian and Western cultures in terms of values, beliefs, and traditions. Young South Asians suggest that the Asian culture comprises *stronger values, beliefs and traditions . . . in terms of religion, and respect of elderly and one another . . . stronger family values and traditions regarding marriage, sex and raising of children [1:5-8].*

Individuals within the Asian culture are taught to respect their elders and have a strict upbringing (*see [8:5-7]*). Furthermore, within the Asian culture, children have closely knitted relationships with their parents (*talking to each other about their problems, eating at the table as a family, helping each other* out . . . *love them for everything they have done for me [7:28-32]*) and are taught to be more focused on a sense of community (see *[4:6-10]*).

Young South Asians are expected to be passive and do not have the right to be heard (*to behave in a certain way . . . in the manner I behave in . . . not voicing your opinion or being open about things [4:32-34]* and (see *[6:10-11]*, *[7:17-20]*, and *[4:33-35]*)). Furthermore, Asian culture encompasses traditional family dynamics of a nuclear family (see *[5:31-33]*), which is given first priority (see *[2:12-13]*). Whereas within the Western culture, family is not given so much importance (see *[6:6]*).

Respondents also proposed that the status of males and females within the Asian culture is not based on equality but male dominance over female. Thus females do not have much say within the family dynamics in comparison with the males (see *[6:34-35]*). The foundation of traditional norms within the South Asian culture stems from their religion that allows children to abide by rules rather than given independence, as they believe that they will follow the wrong pathway in life (*Asian cultures tend to raise their children to believe in their religion and therefore have certain norms and rules to follow which could be why Asian children are not associated with crime [5:10-12]*).

Certain subject matters within the Asian culture such as dating, drinking, certain eating habits, and socialising with friends until late at night are frowned upon (see *[2:11-12]*, *[6:11-13]*, and *[3:20-21]*). This is further supported by Ghuman (1991), who suggests that discussion regarding the opposite sex and dating is restricted within the Asian culture; however, within the Western culture, it is seen as acceptable behaviour.

Nevertheless, respondents tend to disagree with the notion of relationship and marriage within the Asian culture (*my family and I disagree, in terms of their opinions about relationships and marriage where they do not believe in serial dating . . . I believe that I need to get to know different people . . . settle down with [9:8-12]*). Young South Asians suggest that marriage is time dependent whereas the first generation believe that marriage is age dependent (see *[9:12-14]*). The first generation believe that there is a certain age when one should get married whereas the second generation suggest that there is no fixed age, but one should only get married if they are ready.

In addition, the respondents believe that the Western culture is more openly accepted to such subject matters in comparison with the Asian culture (see *[6:5-7]*). Thus it is not surprising that young South Asians want to adapt to Western values, as they are exposed to westernisation and urbanisation (Schoeneman's, 1997).

Furthermore, respondents suggest that the Asian culture gives importance to perfectionism (see *[4:13-14]*) whereas the Western culture gives importance to trial and error (*western culture is more lenient and gives space to individuals to make their own choices and gives space for mistakes [4:12-13]*). This may be due to the 'shame-based' culture that the Asian culture portrays, hence health issues such as disability are looked down upon (*Since I am disabled that either someone else who is disabled will marry me or no one at all, [7:15-16]*). Individuals within the Asian culture are more concerned with the perceptions of others within the society, specifically one's extended family (*constantly get compared to my cousin . . . got an A [4:29-31]*). However, the young South Asians disagree with this (see *[4:27-28]*) and agree with the Western values of seeing each individual as different without any constant comparison.

Due to the differences in expectations and norms within the Asian and Western cultures (see *[9:4-5]*), young south Asian face 'culture clash' and find it hard balancing between the two cultures. The possession of both cultures has led young South Asians experiencing confusion of belongingness due to the pressures that they face living in the Western nation (*these differ nces sometimes puts pressures on the second generation . . . because we are torn between where we come from and where we are actually being raised which happens to be in the western culture [1:8-10]*). This finding coincides with a previous finding by Ghuman (1991), who proposed that during adolescence, South Asians question which culture they belong to when trying to find a place within the Western society (*I do want to follow my family values and traditions, but the social pressure of the western society makes it difficult to know where to turn [1:12-13]*).

Respondents further suggest that they are losing their roots and find it hard to maintain the collectivist ties within the Western culture (see *[3:11-14]*). Hence respondents experience problems with adjusting to the two different worlds (*come home they feel . . . clash in our thoughts [4:21-22]*). This puts pressure on the second generation to choose between the two cultures to which they belong to (*pressure as to which side to choose [1:11-12]*). In relation to this, Ghuman

(1991) proposed that finding a balance between the two differing principle systems is stressful for South Asians; as one cannot be his/her own self. As mentioned earlier, within the Asian culture, parents are concerned about their children's future, as the foundation of the Asian culture is being *inter*dependent (*parents will always support their children till the last day [8:7-8]*) whereas within the Western culture, parents provide support to their children, but to a certain degree, and emphasise more on self-reliance (*western culture . . . support their children but expect the children to be on their own two feet (independent) by the age of 18 . . . move out [8:9-11]*). Thus parents within the Asian culture support their children until they establish a secure future.

Young South Asians seek for independence and disagree with the notion of *inter*dependence due to what they perceive around them within the Western culture (see *[4:25-2]* and *[4:39-41]*. Respondents suggest that if everything is provided for them by their family, they will never learn *[4:24-25]*. This is further supported by Ghuman (1991), who mentions that individuals within their youth want to pull away from their parents to seek independence to search for their identity; however, it is difficult for South Asians to achieve this, as they are bounded by their collectivist culture.

Furthermore, respondents suggest that the first generation see Western values of being independent as immoral (*being independent is seen as . . . is not in the Asian culture that is what I am told [4:64-64]*) for the reason that they want to keep their traditional values alive and pass them on to their children (see *[2:1-2]*).

Nevertheless, respondents acknowledge the importance of internalising traditional values and beliefs, but at the same time, they do not view Western values as necessarily immoral (see *[1:22]*). Respondents mention that their parents need to realise that it is only natural for them to be influenced by the culture in which they are brought up in terms of behaviour and attitude (see *[1:20-22]*).

On the other hand, those young South Asians who have been given the independence of moving out during university establish themselves as independent thinkers (see *[9:22-25]*), hence finding it extremely difficult when their parents intervene and impose their views (*parents get involved . . . want to intervene with issues that I can handle on my own* and (see *[9:25-27]* and *[27-29]*). This finding corresponds with Bhugra (2004), who claims that when young South Asians come across a subject matter, their parents get involved as the Asian culture emphasises on the notion of family unity.

Overall, conclusions drawn out from the respondents' accounts correspond with Ghuman (1991), who proposes that young South Asians do not agree with certain collectivist values such as dating before marriage, everything done should be obeyed by immediate and extended family, and being *inter*dependent. Young South Asians believe that the Asian culture possesses traditional values whereas the Western culture is concerned with progressive values (*Eastern culture try to preserve tradition the western world seem to go with the flow and change with the times . . . two cultures [9:6-8]*).

Generation Gap

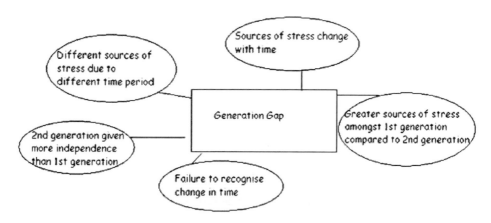

Fig. 10. Codes emerged from theme (generation gap)

Respondents suggested that the difference in perception between the first and second generations is due to the different sources of stress that both the generations face, which is a result of generation gap (see *[6:18-22]*).

Young South Asians acknowledge that the first generation have encountered additional sources of stress, as they had no social support when migrating whereas the second generation have their parental support (see *[9:17-19]*). Respondents also acknowledge that they are given some freedom to make some of their choices in comparison with the first generation when they were young adults (see *[9:21-22]*). Hence, they are given the opportunity to some degree of escaping from interdependence and gain independence as exposed to the westernisation and urbanisation (Schoenman, 1997).

Nevertheless, second generation believe that all sources of stress should be given same importance, and the only difference is that they differ with time. Therefore, parents and children face different sources of stress but are as important as each other (*stresses and situations move with time and therefore stresses that we face today our parents did not have to face [9:20-21]*).

Furthermore, respondents suggest that parents fail to recognise a change in time (*at my age my parents were married with their second child . . . fail to comprehend that we are a different generation and there is change . . . a barrier that differentiates our beliefs [9:14-17]*). Young South Asians suggest that it would be healthier for parents to absorb some of the individualistic values and not completely disregard them, as they could be a learning source (Orozco &-Orozco, 2001). Overall, both generations need to come to a compromise to ensure a healthy well-being (Ranu, 2007).

Family Dynamics

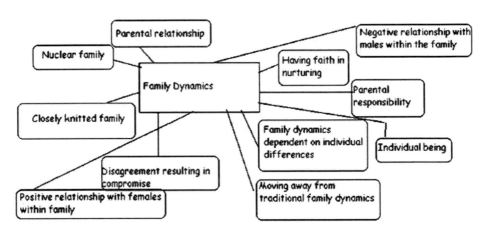

Fig. 11. Some codes emerged from theme (family dynamics)

The Asian culture comprises having closely knitted family dynamics (see *[9:33-34], [8:33-34],* and *[6:36-37]*). South Asians emphasise the notion of community as their identity (Schoeneman, 1997). However, being exposed to urbanisation within the Western culture, traditional family structures are collapsing, leaving individuals engaging within their separate lives and losing a sense of community (see *[9:35-36]*).

Furthermore, South Asians are moving away from traditional family dynamics where the status of women and men within a household is changing with fathers also becoming carers (see *[5:37-41]*).

Nevertheless, within some South Asian families, the traditional family structure of male dominance over female still remains. South Asian females' opinions are not given much importance (see *[6:16-17]*). Hence some South Asian females feel close to their mothers, as being a female they understand the relative status they have within the family dynamics themselves (see *[6:32-34]*).

Furthermore, respondents comment on their ideal family, which comprises a nuclear family (see *[8:27-28]*) that results in disagreement shortly followed by compromise (see *[8:29-31]*). At the same time, young South Asians believe that a nuclear family is not ideal for all, as it depends on the individual's circumstances, e.g. marital satisfaction *[5:33-35]*.

Respondents also suggest that it is the parents' responsibility to bring up their child and teach them the norms of right from wrong *[1:23-25]* and *[1:31-33]*. However when children become older, parents should have enough faith in their nurturing and trust their children to make their own decisions. This is congruent with Ghuman's (1991) assertion that young South Asians want to pull away from their parents to search for their self-identity.

Psychological Well-being

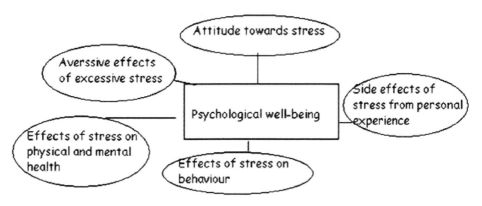

Fig. 12. Some codes emerged from theme (psychological well-being)

Another theme that has emerged through the online surveys was psychological well-being in which respondents mentioned the effects of stress on their attitude, behaviour, and both physical and mental health. Stress affected the second generation's attitude negatively (see *[5:43]*) in which they were unable to approach a subject matter with a clear and constructive mind (see *[9:38-39]*).

The negative attitude consequently had an effect on the individual's behaviour that led the young South Asians feeling *angry [5:43], nervous [3:40], quiet [3:40], anxious [9:37],* and *engage in impulsive behaviour* (see *[9:37]*). However, sometimes respondents isolated themselves from others (*I close myself . . . with my parents [4:65-67]*) or engage in inappropriate behaviour intentionally without considering others' emotions (*don't care about other . . . what they feel and often do things which can upset others [5:44-45]*. Severe stress led the second generation suggesting individuals engaging in inappropriate behaviour such as *smoking [5:46], self-harm [5:44],* and *committing crime or suicidal attempts [5:4-5].*

Research indicates high rates of depression and suicidal attempts amongst the Asian population due to the stress they experience from keeping a balance between the 'culture clash' (Assisi, n.d). In terms of health, stress affects the second generation both physically and mentally. Respondents suggest that they feel physically *worn out [6:47],* lose their appetite *[6:46-47]* and have inadequate sleep, as they are constantly thinking about the stressful situation *[9:39-40].* This is further supported by Wibe et al. (1986), who suggested that excessive sources of stress lead to anxiety and interfere with health-related behaviour such as poor sleep and diet. Stress had physiological effects on the second generation with increasing heart rate (see *[4:69]*), muscle tension, a low immune system, and back pain (see *[7:35-36]*). Mentally, young South Asians feel that they have a cluster of thoughts in their head, which need to be sorted as this affects them to think constructively *[9:1-3].*

Coping Method

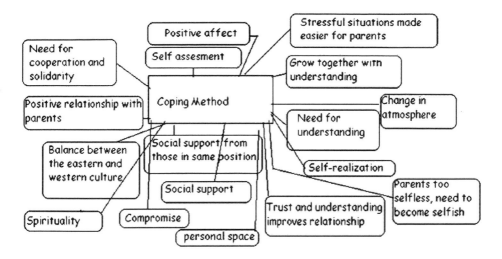

Fig. 13. Some codes emerged from theme (coping method)

Coping method was the final theme that emerged from the respondents' accounts. Similar to the first generation, the theme is divided into two sub-headings. Overall, young South Asians use positive effect (*my attitude . . . tackle the stress* and *I feel I learn from each cause . . . stressful approach [3:40-42]* and *[43-45]*, self-assessment of the stressful situation (*assess the situation [1:40]*), and social support as their main coping methods (see *[9:41]* and *[1:40-43]*). Positive effect and self-assessment allow the respondents to use primary and secondary appraisals that enable them to think with a constructive mind (Lazarous and Cohen, 1973).

As South Asian families are closely knitted and the concern and need for others is emphasised within the Asian culture (Schoeneman, 1997), some respondents therefore use their parents as a form of support when stressed. This is because young South Asians suggest that their parents are able to understand their concerns due to the 'culture clash' they experience (see *[2:18-20]*). Hence young South Asians when stressed find it beneficial to gain social support from those who are in a similar position to them (see *[2:24-25]*). Perhaps South Asians feel that they are unable to get the appropriate support from their Caucasian counterparts due to a lack of understanding with regards to their cultural background (Burningham, 2001).

The second generation find expressing themselves as a form of release from the overloaded stress that they are unable to tolerate (*I have a limit and sometime I let things out if I have bottled them up for a while [8:46-47]*). Respondents also prefer a change in atmosphere (see *[8:35-37]*), require personal space (see *[5:52]*), and use spirituality (see *[7:38]*) to cope.

In order to reduce the levels of stress that arises within the South Asian family dynamics, respondents propose the need for cooperation and solidarity (*to me an ideal family would have beliefs, values, and traditions that have been generated together within the family. Nothing that has been pressured onto children [1:18-20]*) and the need for a balance between the two different cultures (*one which grows and changes accordingly to time but . . . preserve tradition so that the family do not lose their roots and identity [9:33-34]*) (see *[4:53-58]*). Furthermore, young South Asians emphasise on the need for a better understanding amongst parents, as they want to preserve their traditional values and move on with progressive values (see *[9:29-31]*).

Nevertheless, respondents acknowledge that the second generation need to understand the sources of stress that their parents have encountered and place themselves in their parents' position (see *[6:23-25]*).

Respondents noted the importance of compromising in which parents need to acknowledge the influence of the Western values and not impose their views on their children. Simultaneously, children need to respect their parents and not abuse the independence given to them (see *[6:28-32]*).

Overall trust and understanding is the basis of a secure relationship for the first- and second-generation South Asians in the UK (see *[6:26-28]*). Both can take Western values as a source of learning (Bhugra, 2004) and maintain a balance between the two differing cultures (Orozco &-Orozco, 2001).

Summary

The present study focuses on the impact of culture on the first- and second-generation South Asians' perceptions of stress. Previous literature and the present data, which have been reviewed and analysed, have demonstrated how migration and 'culture clash' can have a distressing effect on the lives of the South Asian population.

This study explored the experiences and perceptions of both the generations' sources of stress. The results have established the following:

i. The foundation of both first and second generations' sources of stress is 'culture clash', leading to a difference in perceptions between the first and second generations, hence affecting one's family dynamics. Both generations find it challenging to find a balance between the two differing cultures.

ii. First generation's current source of stress revolves around their children. This includes bringing up their children within the Western culture and providing financial support to settle them with a secure future. Second generation's source of stress is the lack of independence, control, and restrictions they have. This limits them from making their own decisions, as they parents decide what is right from wrong. Second generation suggest that parents should teach their children the rules of right and wrong and have faith on their nurturing.

iii. First generation put strict expectations on their children, hence emphasise the importance of education due to the hardship they experienced with a lack of education. Second generation acknowledge this however want space to experience growth and independence.

iv. Second generation propose that you should 'do what you want to do, not what you should do or is expected of you'. The first generation suggest this is easier said than done, as they are bounded by the collectivist values, which emphasises the concern and need for others and to let go of one's personal goals for the benefit of the group. First generation south Asians are concerned with their children bringing shame to the family. This is based on the perceptions of those within the community ('what will they think or what will they say').

v. First generation argue that the second generation do not understand the value of hardship. This can be questioned, as parents provide everything for their children and give less independence hence reduce the opportunity for their children to learn.

vi. First generation acknowledge that their past source of stress is caused by the rigid Asian values and traditions. Therefore, one can argue the need to replace the collectivist values that cause psychological distress with Western values for a healthy parent-child relationship, since the first generation do not want the second generation to live through the same suffering.

vii. There is a lack of understanding between both parents and children. The first generation propose that their children are depicted to a lot of individualism hence exposed to social pathology. Perhaps the first generation compare the amount of individualism that they were exposed to when their children's age. Nevertheless, the second generation suggest that they are exposed to large amounts of collectivism leading them to sacrifice their personal freedom. They feel that South Asians back home are changing with time adapting to the western culture portrayed on Tv and through technology. However their parents are still stuck in their old ways and adamant to not adapt to the western culture.

viii. Psychological distress experienced by both generations is affecting their attitude, behaviour, and health negatively.

ix. All sources of stress should be given the same importance. The only dissimilarity is that they differ with time.

x. The impact of Western culture has led traditional family dynamics and structures collapsing, leading to healthy relationship indicating the importance of equality and justification for refusal rather than imposing views.

xi. Recommendations have been made by both first and second generations to reduce psychological conflict within one's family dynamics. This includes voicing your opinion rather than suffering in silence and having the ability to contend oneself when wrong despite being older.

Limitations of the Present Study and Strategies/Suggestions for the Future Research

All the responses were collected through an Internet web site made from scratch. As the survey was made available online, this method of data collection neglected the South Asian population who are computer illiterate or who do not have access to a computer. Furthermore, the information displayed on the Internet may not be accurate as it is not at face value; hence deception and accuracy need to be considered.

A suggestion for future research would be to interview or run focus groups to get a fuller understanding of the topic. In addition, it would be appealing to get views of respondents who are above fifty years of age such as South Asians in residential care homes. Also it would be fascinating to get respondents to individually participate in a discussion group online in which they will be asked to discuss the issues that are raised by both the generations in the online surveys (issues that are raised by the first generation that complements the second generation and vice versa). The discussion board online can be used as a form of support group/intervention. This can provide clarification of the respondents' accounts. Furthermore, when analysing the data, it would be beneficial to ask the respondents to participate in analysing their own accounts.

Recommendations

Although the online accounts differ amongst the first and second generations, there are several issues that are acknowledged by both generations. These issues need to be equally considered by the South Asians and health professionals for a healthy well-being amongst the South Asian population. The findings from the present study have implications for the future direction of health psychology in helping health professionals to understand the challenges that can arise when living in two different worlds. This will give health care professionals the opportunity to gain a better understanding of the South Asian population, thus able to deal and communicate well with their needs.

Finally this will enhance the understanding addressed to the South Asian society between the two generations due to the 'culture clash they face'. Therefore the following recommendations can be provided.

1. *Promote being independent without wearing away a sense of community.* As proposed in this study, too much collectivism can lead South Asians to sacrifice their personal freedom. However, too much individualism can lead individuals to engage in social pathology (Bhugra, 2004). Thus a balance is required between the two differing cultures. This can be achieved by the second generation learning to value their Eastern culture and the first generation learning to value the Western culture, creating a necessary balance for healthier relationships and an optimistic mental attitude (Ranu, 2007).

2. *Ensure a better understanding of both the Western and Eastern cultures.* Psychological conflict that arises from culture clash can be reduced by expanding the collectivist value system, as individuals are living within the Western nation (Weinreich, 1996). It would be healthier

for first-generation South Asians to see some aspects of the Western culture as a source of learning rather than discarding it completely (Orozco &-Orozco, 2001). This corresponds with the findings from the present study in which the first generation perceive Western values as immoral. Young South Asians do not want to disregard the collectivist culture but maintain the values from their home culture and adapt to certain British social customs (Orozco &-Orozco, 2001). Also Individuals within the Western culture need to understand the levels of stress associated with migration. This will help facilitate the well-being of the migrants as well as the receiving society.

3. *Health professionals need to be culturally sensitive.* The theoretical emphasis in psychology has been on Caucasian individuals, and studies on the South Asian population have been rare (Maclachlan, 1997). Given the findings from the present study, South Asian individuals are failing to get the appropriate help as there is a lack of understanding of the South Asian background and the individual needs (Burningham, 2001). Hence, South Asians find it more comfortable talking to their peers and family who are from the same ethnicity, as they feel they are better understood. Health services need to be culturally sensitive and trained on aspects of Asian culture to gain a better understanding of the South Asian population, as it is impossible to inflict Western psychology on non-Western problems (Maclachan, 1997).

CHAPTER 3

Appendix

Selection Process

In order to get access to my participants who fit well with my research, I went through a selection process. Through goggle I searched for South Asian support groups, healthy living centres, Asian community networks, and university organisations. I came across several Asian community networks and Asian societies. This online search outlined a list of possible organisations that I could approach for my research.

Nevertheless, I had two different target groups (first and second generations), thus I had to undergo a selection criterion in which I put the organisations into three groups: (1) organisations or networks that target the first generation, (2) organisations and networks that target the second generation, and finally, (3) organisations and networks that target both the first and second generations. Furthermore, I arranged the list of organisations and networks in each group in a hierarchy in terms of order of importance (which best fit with my research).

Finally I went through a process of selection and rejection in which I made two lists (organisations and networks for first and second generations) of the top organisations and networks that I was hoping to approach. This process narrowed down my choices, where I was left with two online networks for my second generation (hi5 and Facebook) and eight for my first generation (Asian family counselling services, South Asian counselling services, Hasting all nation support centre, Asian family consultation service, South Asian society, West London Asian society, Asian health agency, and Asian resource centre Croydon).

In order to access my first generation, I found the contact information for each of my organisations and sent an e-mail to the majority with a letter and my research proposal enclosed via attachment. For those without an e-mail address, I contacted them via phone asking the organisations to mention my study to their clients and ask if they are willing to share their views/thoughts with me. The clients were also told that the online survey will not require much effort from the participants. Also participating in this study may also be therapeutic for them by allowing them to express themselves anonymously online. Organisations were told that in return for their time and participation, I will give them and their clients (1) acknowledgement for their collaboration and (2) co-ownership of the theories and insights generated from this research.

In terms of my second generation, participants from hi5 and Facebook were recruited by creating a discussion board group online. The name of my discussion board group was British Asians in London (second generation). As hi5 and Facebook are global networks, I had to be precise with my group name. In the discussion board group, I outlined the focus of my research project and my web site link for the young generation to click on to, in order to participate in my study. I tried to be informal and posted several messages to prompt second generation South Asians to participate in the study and also thanking those who participated.

Online Survey

First Generation

1. What is stress according to you?
2. How do South Asians perceive stress?
3. Reflect on the changes that you encountered when migrating to this country in terms of

   (a) Social network
   (b) Social status
   (c) Communication
   (d) Values/beliefs and customs

4. From your experience, what kind of sources of stress did you go through being migrated from South Asia to Britain? (Please feel free to give some insight on your thoughts and feelings.)
5. From your experience, what were your sources of stress in the context of family and social dynamics?
6. Do you feel that there is a difference between the way you perceive stress and the second generation in the context of family and social dynamics? (Feel free to elaborate on your experiences.)
7. How do you perceive an 'ideal family'?
8. In comparison with your 'ideal family', reflect on you relationship with your children.
9. From your experience, how does stress affect your

   (a) Behaviour
   (b) Attitude towards the way you perceive things
   (c) Health status

10. How do you cope with stress?

Second Generation

1. What is stress according to you?
2. From your experience, are there any differences between your culture (Asian background) and the Western culture in terms of values, beliefs, and traditions?
3. Do you feel that there is a difference between the way you and the first generation perceive stress in the context of family and social dynamics?
4. In your opinion, what kind of pressures do you face within your family and lifestyle?
5. How do you perceive an 'ideal family'?
6. In comparison with your 'ideal family', reflect on you relationship with your parents.
7. From your experience, how does stress affect your

   (d) Behaviour
   (e) Attitude towards the way you perceive things
   (f) Health status

8. How do you cope with stress?

Consent Form for Research Participations

Cultural Perceptions of Stress amongst First- and Second-Generation South Asians in England

The present study is a requirement for the MSC Health Psychology programme, Department of Psychology, School of Social Science, City University. Your task in this study will consist of participating in an online research survey. You will be required to answer the questions and will be asked to elaborate on your answers with some detail, and you will receive a debriefing slip. Your participation is completely voluntary and does not involve payment.

You are free to withdraw from the study at any time you choose. This study is not expected to involve risk of discomfort or harm. In the event of discomfort or harm, contact numbers are attached. To preserve confidentiality, the results of this study will be coded in such a way that your identity will not be physically attached to the final data produced. I have read and understood the above information. I have had an opportunity to ask questions and I have received answers. I consent to participate in this experiment.

Debriefing

The aim of this study is to demonstrate the understanding of the challenges that can arise from living in two different worlds. This is because the conflict between Asian culture and the British culture can be a source of anxiety for both South Asian parents migrated to Britain and their children who are either born or brought up in Western nations. This study will look at the sources of stress that Asian individual's from the first- and second-generations face, living in Britain in order to enhance the well-being of such individuals. After data collection, an analysis will be performed. The findings of the analysis will be available on the web site. Please ask if you have any further questions.

Thank you for your participation,

Sangeeta Bhalla
Contact details: Sangeeta Bhalla
E-mail address: *abcj789@city.ac.uk*

Phases of Thematic Analysis

The stages involved in thematic analysis include the following:

- *First stage*—Researcher familiarises herself with the data.
- *Second stage*—Reading and rereading of the text. The researcher comments on his/her first impressions of the text, which include initial thoughts and observation.
- *Third stage*—Identification of initial codes across the data set. The researcher collates the data that are relevant to each code, which describe sections of the text. Such codes grasp the quality of what is characterised by the text.
- *Fourth stage*—searching for themes by clustering the codes identified in stage three into potential themes by looking at the association between one another. The cluster of codes will be given labels, which grasp the fundamental nature of the clustered codes hence gathering all the data that are relevant to each potential theme. Some of these themes will be clustered together whereas others will be illustrated by a hierarchical association with another.
- *Fifth stage*—Review the themes to check if the themes work in relation to the coded accounts and the entire data set.
- *Final stage*—Formation of the report that will include selection of quotations from the accounts to support the codes and themes generated from the data, reflecting back on to the analysis in relation to the research questions and literature leading to producing a report of the analysis (Braun & Clarke, 2006).

Reflection of My Experience When Carrying Out Thematic Analysis

My experience with thematic analysis as a method of analysis was knowledgeable. This provided me with the opportunity to analyse my participants' accounts with a different approach from using the usual statistical analysis. Using thematic analysis allowed me to understand and explore the participants' personal experience in depth rather than using a quantitative method that would have summarised the participants' experiences in terms of numerical values. Thematic analysis considers individual differences, as it identifies that different factors contribute to the differences in people's personal experiences.

Furthermore, thematic analysis allowed me to be more creative and flexible, hence play an active role in the research. In order to gain an insider's perspective, I had to describe, analyse, and report patterns within my participants' accounts to make sense of their personal experiences. This allowed me to understand and question my participants' feelings and thoughts regarding their experiences.

Furthermore, the themes that emerged within the data allowed me to sum up the significant features of a large body of data and generated unexpected insight. Nevertheless, thematic analysis was a challenge, as I had never used it before; I had to be careful with what I was doing, as I did not want the analysis to be biased with my beliefs. Since the analysis gives the opportunity of flexibility and creativity, it was hard to separate my views from my participants, as I had to analyse their experiences, thus the analysis had my conceptions of the participants' personal experience. To overcome such barriers, *reliability* (the extent to which my measuring procedure yields the same results on repeated trials) and *validity* (the extent to which the method of analysis used is truly measuring what I intended to measure) tests were considered (Heffner, 2004). These included the following:

1. Use of quotations from the participants' accounts to support the codes and themes that were generated from the data
2. Constant comparison—comparing data between and amongst participants to see saturation when it happens and also this helps in bringing up gaps in participants' data
3. Participants' accounts were used to cross-validate my findings from the thematic analysis. This was used as conformability to demonstrate the neutrality of the research interpretations
4. Peer debriefing—having my South Asian peers review the analysis along the process helped me identify the gaps and discrepancies that I might not otherwise have found. An outsider's perspective often brings other things to light. If the interpretation is similar with others, then it improves its credibility (Heffner, 2004).

Overall, thematic analysis is a beneficial method as it explores an individual's experience in depth, and such human behaviour is difficult to understand in greater depth by using numerical values. However, as thematic analysis is a flexible, creative, and time-consuming method since you have to reread through the text several times to capture the essence, as the quality of the participants' account is dependent on the quality of the analysis, many researchers are reluctant to use this. However, thematic analysis presents a more accessible form of analysis for those with limited experience within the qualitative field and is a quick method to learn (Braun & Clarke, 2006).

Effect on the Reader

There was a similarity between the majority of the accounts analysed. The accounts portrayed moving stories regarding the individual's experiences and feelings. Being a South Asian myself, I could understand the psychological issues that are raised by both the first and second generations. It was striking to see the changes that the first generation encountered when migrating to England and the tragedies they faced associated with such changes. It made me feel that sometimes the second generation take what they have for granted. At the same time, the second generation feeling that they are torn into two different worlds and experience a confusion of belongingness makes me question the beliefs of the collectivist culture, which emphasises 'the concern and need for others'.

CHAPTER 4

South Asians Today

British Asian Women and Alcohol

Drinking alcohol was not predominately accepted in earlier generations. Nevertheless, it has been associated with British Asian men for many years. Today the trend is being shifted with the new generation. Some British Asian women use alcohol as one of the measures to highlight a change in social status. Alcohol was once a representation of male dominance over female, but due to a change in lifestyle, more personal freedom, financial independence, and increased socialisation, this image has become a reflection of the past. This is evident with many British Asian women drinking at weddings and social functions openly now, which is something that was not so common a decade ago in the UK. This shows that it is now being accepted as a way of life than in the past amongst both sexes.

However, some British Asian girls have misused this notion. There has been an increase in excessive alcohol consumption amongst British Asian girls who benefit from night-outs during university or college times. It is reasonable to understand that it is sometimes difficult to control a habit, but one can assume that these young women are beginning to abuse their contemporary established freedom. 'Seeing a young Brit-Asian girl, possibly in her early twenties, very drunk, slightly conscious, lying on her back alone on the footpath, next to a pool of vomit in front of a public cinema entrance, is not exactly the picture that would be a respectful advert for the Brit-Asian youth and culture of today' (Nazat, 2003). Studying, living, or working away from their controlled or strict family environments encourages them to continue with this behaviour.

Nevertheless, peer pressure may have an effect where drinking plays an influential role. The idea of British Asian females do not drink or have very little in comparison with their peers of other races in the UK is misconstrued. Many young British Asian girls have admitted that being under the influence of excessive alcohol consumption, 'they did not know what they did, where they went, and some engaged in sexual intercourse without being in control of with whom and where'. Even so, there are some British Asian women who do not agree with drinking, as they feel that they do not need to in order to enjoy themselves, but they are no longer the majority they once were. Some Asian families disregard females drinking, as they associate it with a loss of identity of the Asian culture. However, newer and younger generations of British Asians do not share the same views. Asian women drinking alcohol is not viewed as immoral in this day and age but having control of your actions and not drinking excessively leading to loss of self-control, consciousness, and respect for your own body need to be brought to attention. Individuals need to steer clear of the gender divide concept with alcohol consumption viewed as being masculine for males but derogatory for females.

Premarital Sex and British Asian Women

> *Darkness; complete and utter, no sound.*
> *Drowned.*
> *Sparks, shards of light; run, bounce, up and down,*
> *Illuminate Dad's frown.*
> *His stare.*

Then glare,
From the lights make shapes dance,
Across my eyes,
Create in me,
A trance-like state,
Designed to keep me here.
Locked in fear.

They'll never understand,
Outside of marriage, unplanned;
A one night stand,
Which led to my shame,
So taboo.
Caught up in this game.

Lost respect,
I shall never escape or forget but regret,
And now I close my eyes,
And realise;
I'm torn.

Copyright Rhiann Pryor 2011

Premarital sex, unplanned pregnancies, one-night stands, and single mothers are phrases that have become common use within the Asian culture today. Nevertheless, they still remain controversial topics, as most Asians from the first generation view premarital sex as bringing shame to their family. Keeping your virginity is highly valued within the South Asian culture.

It signifies purity and chaste and having respect for oneself. Women are expected to uphold their traditional values. They are expected to look after the men in their lives and that often means sacrificing for them. Women are placed in a submissive role in these relationships, often being coerced into sexual relationships. Families have seemed to be a complication. The situation where the man has not told his family about his girlfriend and subsequently splits up with her due to family pressure is common. Nonetheless, the Western mindset has brought changes to these preserved cultural values. The independent British Asian woman is now making more decisions for herself. The new lifestyle is allowing her to decide on matters such as sexual relationships. With marriages happening later in life due to careers and personal choices, the desire to have dating relationships, and subsequently sex before marriage, is becoming a growing factor amongst younger generations of British Asians.

Statistics confirm that there is an increase in sex before marriage amongst British Asian woman from independent women to those that have secret sexual relationships. This image has been portrayed in the popular TV programme 'Coronations Street', where actress Sunita Parekh plays the role of a single mother signifying the new sexually independent Asian woman. Research studies including one conducted by the national Teenage Pregnancy Unit concludes that British Asians have become more sexually liberated. Young British Asians (second generation) were more likely than their parents to engage in premarital sex within secret relationships.

Nevertheless, the vast majority of girls within the Asian community are inhibited by family considerations and are not liberal towards premarital sex. Secret relationships, fear of being found out, and illicit affairs are still a major part of British Asian life. Keeping sexual activity confined to secrecy and having non-public relationships are still the way for many British Asian women. Unwanted pregnancy as a result of not using effective contraception during premarital sex is becoming more common and an issue for young British Asian women. While being confused with subjects such as dating and sex, Young British Asians are subjected to extra pressure of going through the experience in isolation and keeping it from their parents or supportive networks, making them more vulnerable. These women would seek an abortion if they became pregnant. Their parents would force them to marry if they were caught.

BBC Asian Network reports that there is a rise in British Asian women having abortions. The numbers have increased from 10,084 in 2003 to 15,197 in 2007. Surveys confirm that many of them are in consented sexual relationships. Attitudes and behaviour towards premarital sex within the Asian populations are changing dramatically. Young British Asians are growing up in a society where issues such as sexual activity and relationships are discussed freely, and the figures mentioned above support this.

The media including *Bollywood* plays a vital role in portraying images of sexually confident Asian women. These images have become more explicit over time. The stereotype of the demur Asian Women has faded with the rise of the images of sexually independent women. This has created expectations of Asian women to be sexually liberated (Basu, 2009). Nevertheless, music, fashion, films, and club culture also play a part. A significant proportion of British Asian youth are influenced by the music culture such as listening to urban RnB, hip hop, and Garage music. The music portrays under-dressed women flaunting their sexuality, raunchy dance moves, and sexually predatory men. Most Asian women are exposed to alcohol, smoking, and drugs in a clubbing environment. This makes them more vulnerable, hence more likely to engage in risky sexual behaviour. Peer pressure and social groups are dictating sexual attitudes.

Gender differences are strong within the South Asian culture. Women are brought up to believe they need a man in their lives. Men see themselves as superior and are not given guidance in sexual matters. This creates an imbalance of power. It increases one-night stand behaviour and promiscuity in men, putting women in a vulnerable position in relationships where they are more likely to be used and become single mothers. A culture that places importance on female virginity and is more lenient on men creates double standards in behaviour. Women stand to lose more from a sexual liaison and are more likely to be treated with disrespect. The South Asian culture is going through a transition from traditional ideas of relationships to a relaxed liberal outlook on sex. There needs to be an acknowledgement that young people's values and lifestyles have changed, and gender difference should not persist. Premarital sex has become more accepted by the young British Asian population. Nevertheless, one should not abuse this as it is disrespectful/degrading to oneself and the risks (STD and HIV) associated with having multi-partners.

Young British Asians from both sexes need support and guidance more than anything else, as the incidence of unwanted pregnancies has increased. A campaign targeting British Asians to raise awareness of risky sexual behaviour is needed. Messages of safe sex apply to British Asians as much as anyone else. It is not just contraception advice that is required. Attitude and behavioural changes need to be explored to encourage more informed choices.

Loss of Traditions or Making the Best of Both Worlds?

Traditions are passed on through generations. First-generation South Asians migrating to the UK have held on to their traditions, values, and culture to retain their connection to their identity and origin while seeking a new life in a Caucasian-dominated country. Many South Asians may have not expected to stay but sent money back home with the aim of returning.

Nevertheless, majority of the South Asian population have built their life from scratch within the UK, upholding their traditional values. As some decided to stay, the second generation known as British Asians were born, who have accepted the UK as their home while maintaining the Asian values and culture. It is generalised that British Asians are losing many traditions brought over to the UK by their parents and grandparents. However, it is not losing traditions but forming their own identity keeping a balance between the Eastern and Western values.

Second generation find it easier to adapt to the UK in comparison with the first generation, as they have attended British schools and universities, educated themselves, and secured jobs in different industries compared to their parents. The first generation struggled to build a life from scratch working as manual labourers with their qualifications not having much value in the UK. Nevertheless, the integration has led some British Asians losing their values such as not knowing their mother tongue, respect for elders, and the sense of close-knitted families which is highly stressed upon within the Asian culture. British Asians should not be viewed negatively by the South Asian society for adopting Western ways in order to develop an identity for themselves, but at the same time should not forget their roots that form their individuality and uniqueness (Baines, 2009).

'Living in' a Growing Indian Trend

The trend of 'living together' before marriage is growing amongst South Asians in India, the UK, and other countries abroad. The consequence of this change is testing the traditional versus modern way of life. Living together was never an option in the past amongst South Asians (before marriage or instead of marriage) and is still controversial now as subject matters such as dating, premarital sex, and interracial relationships are still looked down upon. Nevertheless, this view has changed for some, where couples are using this as an option, even in India, due to the growing modernisation and urbanisation. This change in habitat between couples compared to the traditional route of living together after marriage is not as easy as it seems to be. It is the definition indeed, which has a lot of loopholes. Is it just living together like two separate entities? Is it sharing of the expenses and eating in or out together? Or is it just like a marriage without the social and legal registration, without a wedding ceremony, a mother-in-law, and the status taken of being a daughter/son-in-law (Kaur, 2009).

Despite the social taboo, couples are defiantly taking the option of 'living in' and sharing lives as single partners and boyfriend/girlfriend. But when circumstances turn unpleasant, it becomes complicated with legal and financial matters, especially when an offspring is born. Second-generation British Asians are adapting these norms from the West using this as an option to check if two individuals could stay together for a lifelong commitment or not.

Nevertheless, the problem lies in how far a living in relationship goes. When individuals get emotionally attached (in some cases, even financially) and physical intimacy is present, then the lines defining the relationship become blurred. Because then the independence of a 'living-in' relationship ceases to exist and what results is a disaster.

Recently in Maharashtra in India, living together before marriage is made legal. If an offspring is a result of this, he/she will be permitted with equal rights towards financial wealth and property. One may question if individuals are so eager for commitment, why not get married? With this proposal, there won't be any difference between a marriage and a 'living-in' relationship. With these relationships not being registered but having the same status of a marriage, problems are bound to arise due to no real clarity of one versus the other. Nonetheless, 'living-in' relationships having a legal standing will remove the social taboos it holds, paving the way to give individual more choice over who they decide to live with and develop relationships.

Marriage—Arranged, Love, or Out of Convenience?

Second-generation South Asians are put under pressure, as they hit the mid-twenties' benchmark. It is automatically assumed that they will have a respectable career and will be 'ready' for marriage, a family, and children, as this is the South Asian way of life. Not forgetting, they need to meet the criteria and tick the correct boxes same religion/culture, caste, as well as the conventional aspects of a relationship that everybody is in search of (finding the right partner who they would want to spend their life with). Those that do not fit the clichéd are looked down upon as it is not seen as 'normal'. Extended families as well as individuals within the society make negative remarks and ask numerous questions whether you are walking down the street or meeting up at a social event, 'So when are you getting married?' One may suspect as second generations are given a 'deadline', are the marriages sometimes out of convenience and seemed rushed into, generating problems in the future?

The concept of arranged marriages has changed significantly, from once where parents arranged their children's marriage without any of their preposition to an eased approach of families allowing the couple to date, get to know each other, and further to decide their future. Nevertheless, in more orthodox families, arranged marriages have been more of a way of life and still remains. Many Asians are becoming more accepting towards love marriage, as it provides an individual the freedom to choose their partner, date, and enter a relationship for whatever period and then involve the families when they feel comfortable to do so. The latter part always can have an impact on the outcome of the relationship ending up in marriage or not. However, religion and race are two factors that have an impact on love marriages.

Mixed marriages of religion amongst South Asian communities can be a challenge. In some cases, one religion may be seen as the leader in the relationship where one partner converts to adapt the lifestyle of the other partner. In other cases, partners respect each other's religion and do not see the need to change. In terms of race, the differences are directly related to culture. The marrying of two cultures in this way usually means that one partner will adopt more or less of the other partner's culture. For example, an Asian girl may neglect her roots and culture and adopt a completely Western way of life if she marries, say British white man and vice versa. Nevertheless, there are couples within interracial relationships who keep a balance and the best of both worlds (Nazhat, 2008).

The general expectation of most South Asian parents is for their child to seek and marry a person from the same background, i.e. culture, religion, and even caste. However, this has changed with interracial marriages becoming increasingly common and the tradition of staying within the boundaries no longer being followed. Traditional families see this change as a 'bad thing' and feel that only parents can find suitable matches. They cannot accept that young Brit-Asians prefer a relationship before marriage and do not want to get married how their parents did (arranged marriage).

Interracial Relationships:

In my culture we hear the dj's say mix and blender,
But I have loved the artistic design of the drawn henna,
On your hand painted, a lighter complexion,
But why should this be the reasons of complication?

Your dad liking me when we were friends,
Found out were together, and that came to an end,
With obstacle in the way, life isn't what it seems,
But when times get tough you must pursue in your dreams.

Been together on and off for three long years,
your family disowning you is what I feared,
never wanted to break up so we've let out many tears-
enough to cry me a river.
But my love to you is what I deliver.

The thought of not being yours makes me shiver,
Watching your parents hook you up with another guy makes me quiver,
I feel so useless, but what can I do?
Punching walls out of frustration but stay strong when with you.

What more can I do, I'm running out of ideas,
Not crying no more, I ain't got no more tears.
And yes, I'm still scared, but it's loosing you that I fear,
We've given our everything, we can't give up now that ware here.

Don't mean to annoy you or make you provoked,
Staying positive together is our only antidote,
There's no need to lie, with you by my side,
We can take on the world like Bonney and Clyde.

When we walked the streets holding hands, people stopped and stared,
So I grabbed and kissed you because I don't really care,
People judging me because I am black,
Get to know me first, then let me hear your chat.

I know this sounds cocky, I'm nice that's a fact,
I can be myself everywhere and anywhere, there's no need to act,
Just hear me out—it shouldn't matter that my skin is black.

I've been independent from my early teens
And that's why I'm special, there was no help in-between.
In the dark, you are my ray of light,
My trapped Indian Princess I'll save you—I'm your dark skinned knight,

What can I do so you can understand me?
My skin is black but I'm still a human being.

Copyright Danny Clarke, 2011

Even though South Asians in India are changing with time with the influence of the economy, modern technology, and Western values, South Asians (first generation) in the UK who have migrated from India are still rigid with their beliefs and values. They have maintained these as they do not want their children to lose sight of their culture. However, they do not recognise that South Asians in India are changing and learning to adapt to Western values. South Asians are being strict with the idea of dating and marriages from the same caste system are becoming more open minded to different casts. South Asians within the UK have also been swayed to this idea.

Nevertheless, they overlook that the UK is a multi-ethnic society, where individuals are not just from different castes within India but from different ethnicities (white, black, and Asian). Hence young South Asians are put under pressure and find it very difficult to date/marry someone not just from the same ethnicity but also from the caste within the Asian culture.

Being exposed to different ethnicities living in the UK, young South Asians find it difficult to abide by the norms and therefore feel the need to hide this from their parents. They understand that perhaps it is difficult to maintain a relationship with someone from a different ethnicity possessing different cultural values/morals/beliefs/lifestyle and traditions but not impossible to merge two different cultures and develop a balance and understanding.

The South Asian community is very hostile towards Asians in a mixed-race relationship. It is a shame as some of the younger generation tend to be more compassionate than their parents/grandparents 'what amazes me the most is that despite a man and a woman falling in love and feeling good about it, family and friends often feel strongly against it just because their racial biases. It is a shame . . . let everyone live up to the saying, is the wearer who knows best where the shoe pinches' (Mzee Safari, 2004).

Asians in interracial relationships find it a hurdle telling their parents and their relationship remains a secret due to cultural and religious differences. It is more difficult for an Asian girl than a boy due to male dominance over female within Asian culture. Interracial relationships are becoming more common in the UK. However, there is still a strong stigma towards relationships between South Asians and those from a different race. South Asians do not agree with interracial relationships due to a difference in culture and religion between two partners. They feel that the children of these individuals will not know which religion or culture to follow and will find it difficult to fit entirely with one race leading to many obstacles, sacrifices, and compromises.

It can be argued that the success of mixed-race relationships depends on the literacy and exposure of the families involved. It has worked in a society where the two families are educated while others are plagued with problems. People should not feel that they need to trade their ethnicity, but if individuals are in an interracial relationship and want it to work, there needs to be an understanding, respect, and balance towards each other's culture. Problems arise when most are not familiar with each other's culture.

One can genuinely express that interracial couples are subjected to all kinds of pressures both internal and societal (I expect people to be more open minded; almost every day is a new challenge. Interracial relationships can be wonderful but the ignorance of some people is a real challenge. When will it change? How many generations do we need to learn that the separation of skin colour is created by ignorant people' (Isha, 2004). Their success depends on economic conditions and interpersonal communication. The prejudice of others can compromise if couples are already on a shaky ground (GMT, 2004).

'Race is a social construct; it is not innate to humanity but rather a tool for conditioning others' (Emmanuel, GMT, 2004). Individuals should be able to form relationships with whom they choose to, bearing in mind their happiness. Interracial relationships can be more challenging, hence understanding, strong foundation between the couple, communication, valuing, and respecting the other person's morals and culture are important. It is nice to see interracial relationships as experiencing the best of worlds and being exposed/welcomed into so many communities. For a child being brought up by mixed-race parents is often asked what culture does he/she feel more comfortable in. What people need to understand is that these children are the product of both cultures.

Divorce Rise amongst South Asian Families

From Duty to Divorce

> *Concrete rules set so clear by time,*
> *Set in stone, a worn out rhyme.*
> *A delightful dance of golden hues and red,*
> *Here a good husband, in general gladness wed.*

Culture encircles, and norms respected,
Self-sacrifice a necessity, doubts rejected.
So arises the burden of certain expectations,
A culture perpetuated, by many generations.

Tolerant, drifting—constant emotional drone,
What justice is life, this dilemma stands alone,
True happiness in marriage, stagnant duty's toil,
Trapped and shaken viciously, from rain of blows recoil.

So begins the internal scream, the children must'nt hear,
Infusions of simmering anger, vision no longer clear.
A midnight lament, the mourning of lost ideals,
Tired soul a blossom, in daily prayer one kneels.

Nights wept away, seek refuge in bed of tears,
Coping day by day, creeping daily fears.
Smouldering frustration, acceptance takes its turn,
Within recess of ones' mind, a rising passion burns.

To live a content life, free from this oppression,
Claustrophobic, according to custom, a marital depression.
Forbidden reaches of happiness, 'tis harder than it seems,
What is life really, if not the pursuit of your dreams?

The beauty of a culture, the tragedy of reality,
Conflicts of emotion, an emerging duality.
Anchor of an ideal, the instinct within,
Melting hesitation, for that which is branded sin.

Indecision, judgement, a fear to not conform,
Divorce is an option, alien to cultures' norm.
Shatter the streak, which many will defend,
But enough is enough, this delusion must end.

In need of grace, relief, from relatives' wrath hide,
Disowned—criticised—wade against a cultures' tide.
Alone, save courage, take the damned step to justice,
Personal pride intact, despite whispered words of malice.

The female injustice, a man's honour pained,
Smiling and weeping, leaving what was gained.
Ideas become malleable, tradition is not dead,
A greater goal of happiness, emerging values fed.

Copyright Marie-Therese Octavia Png, 2011

Once where women had to put up with abusive/violent relationships and had no option to turn to are now acknowledging divorce as a solution. Where marriage was central to the social status of the Indian women, today it is not the case as younger women are breaking the mould and are becoming more intolerant of their partners. Many unhappy women are now taking the stance to leave relationships compared to those of the past that took everything that were willing to tolerate the lot, for the sake and honour of the family/society. Abusive relationships are one key reason for many splits, where the women feel enough is enough. Violent and abusive partners are no longer being tolerated. Families of the women are also becoming more understanding. In general, Indian women today are becoming physically, financially, and sexually more demanding those past generations.

Indian women are educating themselves, choosing professional careers, and becoming more independent, hence raising their expectations of marital life. Financial security and dependency on the man, as once practised in the past, are now no longer the case. Professional women are making their own choices, and financial stability is giving them the confidence, which was not present in the past.

The term 'divorce' does not exist within the Asian Language; nevertheless, it is becoming common amongst South Asians today. Divorce was a much difficult thing to do or accept. The financial and emotional support offered today did not exist then. Women more so than men would not have the courage to leave and would accept whatever the man did in the marriage, e.g. affairs and so forth.

Nevertheless, gender differences still remain. It is an easier option for Asian men in comparison with Asian women to have a divorce, as the stigma of a female divorcee is larger. Men have traditionally been the dominating party seeking divorce and the reasons do not have to be significant. It is easier for a divorced man to find a new partner compared to a divorced woman, especially if the woman also has children. But it is likely that this outlook will potentially change due the growth in the numbers of women who are now divorcing in India.

However, the option for divorce is still class led because the rise is being seen amongst the educated, wealthier middle class. The lower classes still do not see it as an option due to stigma, costs, and the delay in the justice system, which can take years for cases to be settled, especially if they involve children.

Keeping the Status Intact

I'm not allowed tattoos, but I'm allowed henna.
Now I'm looking at my parents like you,
My dad wants me to study law on holidays,
Working in his shop and sell hair and rinju.

There are traditions for a Hindu, Sikh and Muslim culture,
From which we embrace our values, and morals, that shape our future
But now we've come so far, travelled the world, been exposed,
To the West.
We've been influenced, and merged with the rest.

Especially to women, I know freedom's been due: YES.
But that seems like yesterday past tense—I must confess.
Because Dad will disown me,
Mum won't be proud of me: now I'm stressed.

Vexed and feeling brain damaged,
Were no longer in the East—I don't want an arranged marriage.
I've found love in other colours, how do I explain it.
Because the shade's different from mine, they say the loves tarnished—tainted.

Either side I pick I'm removing myself,
I don't just loose out—I'm losing myself.
This is not back home, though I abide by regulations,
I followed rules, lost friends, love, but gained an education.

Staying true to the East, avoiding Western government legislation.
You've planed life for me, so what is my destination?
Living for others who tell me what I should have seen,
Or being me and living what I should of been.

I quote the Quran and try to follow the Sarms,
Never missing a day to hear the words of the Imam.
He says if I don't, I will burn in flames,
Is that a holy command, or what he claims?
But if I do when I rest I will be in Gods arms.
Living a lavish life with Elijah Muham.

It isn't fair. Mans' laws and holy laws.
We can't win mans' wars or holy wars.
Please forgive but are mans' laws holy laws?
In some Eastern countries, these words they would stone me for.
No matter what they may say—I'm still pure.

We were taught to believe only God can judge me.
That's a lie; it's a mans' world in every country.
As a child our minds are programmed and cuffed, you see?
I stepped out of line, now they no longer want me,
It makes me think do you really love me.

Its funny—most will work through their marriage,
Fight through sickness and health. For better or for worst.
That's why it hurts.
I laugh in pain because you won't do the same for your offspring,
Sometimes I think suicide—life is so exhausting.

Some parents are intolerant, and raise their future on tell-lie-vision.
Tell me what's worst—TV or religion.
Don't get it twisted, I love that I'm a part of my culture, religion.
But if I explore other cultures am I no longer an Indian?

Every day I wake up, I thank God for my presence,
But no religion nowadays is in true essence.
Not even the most righteous could disagree with that.
Nope, I'm not pointing fingers I'm pointing out facts.
So despite the soil I was born on, what makes me Indian,
My skin is not much different from Gods' West Indian and African Children.
My hair is more or less as those who are white.
Ok—different accents and morals in life.
Indian or not—we're all the same when you turn off the light.

Life is already hard don't make it any harder
By judging me, yourself, and each other.

Copyright Uhuru Robinson, 2011

Asian families have many expectations of each other due to their collectivist culture which highlights interdependence. This may put a lot of pressure on individuals. Status and reputation are highly valued within the Asian culture, which is dependent on following the traditional principles. Due to the collectivist culture placing importance on interdependence, parents have many expectations of their children to keep their status intact. This can sometimes cause discomfort, as Asian parents may contemplate their children's happiness if it does not comply with their cultural values.

Non-compliance to traditional morals is seen as bringing shame to the family because South Asians' identity is made up of one another, hence the actions of an individual has an effect on the others within the family dynamics. As mentioned earlier that the collectivist culture in which South Asians are raised in puts a lot of emphasis on interdependence and family dynamics, children are brought up with a lot of support from their families especially financial (a higher education, buying a car and a house for them—making sure that they are well settled) in comparison with teenagers within the Western culture who at the age of sixteen are asked to leave home or pay for their living costs. They are seen as independent individuals who need to learn and make decisions, choose to build a future of their own. The South Asian second generation is fortunate to get the support of their parents who tend to love them unconditionally, as they expect nothing in return. Nevertheless, their child needs to condemn to the values and traditions of the South Asian culture, which underlies their reputation that is the pride of the South Asian culture (completing a higher education and getting a reputable job, e.g. something preferably within the field of health care doctor, pharmacist, and so forth and finally marrying within their own religion/caste).

As revealed previously, living within a multi-ethnic society in England, it is very difficult for children to form relationships within their religion/castes. Due to the influence of Western values/traditions, children have formed different concepts to the first generation where they place importance on independence as well as interdependence. They want the freedom to pick and choose their own career, relationships, and their own way of living. However, those that do not condemn to their parents' values have to deal with the guilt that is fed by their families for sacrificing by prioritising their children's needs since birth, e.g. raising them and helping them settle for their future while not expecting anything in return. 'What haven't we done and given you, good education, car, house, clothes, money to go out, anything that you have asked for and the only thing that we are asking of you is to obtain a good career to help you and your family financially in the future and to be with someone from your own culture.' These self-concepts are dependent on having a good reputation amongst society as South Asians are concerned with 'what will people say (lokee ki kehn ge)'. Condemning to the cultural values/traditions is something that does not need to be asked but accepted. So does the unconditional love become conditional as conditions raised are not complied to?

Summary

The issues mentioned above need to be acknowledged without pretence of their non-existence. As some South Asians may believe that if they won't recognise the existence of these issues, there are less chances of their occurrence. But in fact the reality is that these issues do exist, but as they are taboo within the South Asian culture, they are not spoken of. The second generation due to this take on board this attitude, 'what they don't know won't hurt them'. This should not be the case; second generation should be able to talk openly about such issues with their parents, building a stronger bond where parents feel more involved in their child's life, caring less about what people think and say and more about what they think themselves, enhancing understanding and communication. First generation need to adapt to the changes with time if they want to maintain an honest and healthy relationship with their children.

REFERENCES

Astington, J.W. (2003) Sometimes necessary, never sufficient: False-belief understanding and social competence, in Repacholi, B. Slaughter, V. (2003). Individual differences in theory of mind, New York:: Psychology press, pp. 13-38.

Berger, K.S. (2003). The developing person through childhood and adolescence, Worth publishers.

Coolican, H. (2004). Research methods and statistics in psychology, Cambridge university press.

He, Z., Bolz, M. and Baillargeon, R. (2009). False-belief understanding in 2.5-year-olds: evidence from violation-of-expectation change of location and unexpected-contents tasks. *Developmental Sciences, no. doi: 10.1111/j.1467-7687.2010.00980.*

Hughes, C. and Leekam, S. (2004). What are the links between theory of mind and social relations? Review, reflections and new directions for studies of typical and atypical development. *Social Development.13 (4),* pp. 590-619.

Mareschal, D., Quinn, P.C. and Johnson, M.H. (2009). Available at:

http://www.wiley.com/bw/journal.asp?ref=1363-755x [viewed: 29.12.11]

Mary, T. (2004) Social research: issues, methods and process, Open university press.

Onishi, K.H. and Baillargeon, R. (2005). Do 15-month-old infants understand false belief?. *Science, 308 (5719),* pp. 255-258)

Razza, R.A. (2009). Associations among False-belief Understanding, Executive Function, and Social Competence: A Longitudinal Analysis, *Journal applied developmental psychology,* 20 *(3),* pp. 332-343.

Rose, M. and Scott R.B. (2010). Attributing false beliefs about non-obvious properties at 18 months. *Cognitive Psychology 61 (4),* pp. 366-395.

Ruffman, T. (1996). Do children understand the mind by means of stimulation or a theory? Evidence from their understanding of inference. *Mind & Language, 11 (4),* pp. 388-414.

Senju, A. Southgate, V., Miurya, Y., Matsui A.T. and Csibra, G. (2010). Absence of spontaneous action anticipation by false belief attribution in children with autism spectrum disorder. *Development and Psychopathology 22,* pp. 353-360.doi:10.1017/S0954579410000106.

Southgate, V., Chevallier, C. and Csibra, G. (2010). Seventeen—months old appeal to false beliefs to interpret others referential communication. *Developmental sciences 13 (6),* pp. 907-912.

Souhgate, V., Seju, A. and Csibra, G. (2007). Action anticipation through attribution of false belief by 2 year olds. *Psychological science, 18, (7),* pp. 587-592.

Sperber, D. (1994). Understanding verbal understanding. In Southgate, V., Chevallier, C. and Csibra, G. (2010). Seventeen—months old appeal to false beliefs to interpret others referential communication. *Developmental sciences 13 (6),* pp. 907-912.

BIBLIOGRAPHY

Astington, J.W. (2003) Sometimes necessary, never sufficient: False-belief understanding and social competence, in Repacholi, B. Slaughter, V. (2003). Individual differences in theory of mind, New York:: Psychology press, pp. 13-38.

Baillargeon, R., Scott, R.M and He, Z. (2010), False belief understanding in infants, *Trends in Cognitive Sciences, 14 (3),* pp 110-118.

Berger, K.S. (2003). The developing person through childhood and adolescence, Worth publishers.

Carpenter, M., Call, J., and Tomasello, M. (2002). A new false belief test for 36-month-olds. *British Journal of Developmental Psychology, 20, (3),* pp. 393-420.

Csibra, G. (2010). *Recognizing Communicative Intentions in Infancy. Mind and Language 25 (2),* pp. 141-168.

Coolican, H. (2004). Research methods and statistics in psychology, Cambridge university press.

Happe, F. and Loth, E. (2002). 'Theory of mind' and tracking speakers' intentions. *Mind & Language, 17 (1-2),* pp. 24-36.

He, Z., Bolz, M. and Baillargeon, R. (2009). False-belief understanding in 2.5-year-olds: evidence from violation-of-expectation change of location and unexpected-contents tasks. *Developmental Sciences, no. doi: 10.1111/j.1467-7687.2010.00980.*

Hughes, C. and Leekam, S. (2004). What are the links between theory of mind and social relations? Review, reflections and new directions for studies of typical and atypical development. *Social Development.13 (4),* pp. 590-619.

Mareschal, D., Quinn, P.C. and Johnson, M.H. (2009). Available at:

http://www.wiley.com/bw/journal.asp?ref=1363-755x [viewed: 29.12.11]

Mary, T. (2004) Social research: issues, methods and process, Open university press.

Onishi, K.H. and Baillargeon, R. (2005). Do 15-month-old infants understand false belief?. *Science, 308 (5719),* pp. 255-258)

Razza, R.A. (2009). Associations among False-belief Understanding, Executive Function, and Social Competence: A Longitudinal Analysis, *Journal applied developmental psychology,* 20 *(3),* pp. 332-343.

Rose, M. and Scott R.B. (2010). Attributing false beliefs about non-obvious properties at 18 months. *Cognitive Psychology 61 (4),* pp. 366-395.

Ruffman, T. (1996). Do children understand the mind by means of stimulation or a theory? Evidence from their understanding of inference. *Mind & Language, 11 (4),* pp. 388-414.

Senju, A. Southgate, V., Miurya, Y., Matsui A.T. and Csibra, G. (2010). Absence of spontaneous action anticipation by false belief attribution in children with autism spectrum disorder. *Development and Psychopathology 22,* pp. 353-360.doi:10.1017/S0954579410000106.

Southgate, V., Chevallier, C. and Csibra, G. (2010). Seventeen—months old appeal to false beliefs to interpret others referential communication. *Developmental sciences 13 (6),* pp. 907-912.

Souhgate, V., Seju, A. and Csibra, G. (2007). Action anticipation through attribution of false belief by 2 year olds. P*sychological science, 18, (7),* pp. 587-592.

Sperber, D. (1994). Understanding verbal understanding. In Southgate, V., Chevallier, C. and Csibra, G. (2010). Seventeen-months old appeal to false beliefs to interpret others referential communication. *Developmental sciences 13 (6)*, pp. 907-912.

Tomasello, M., and Harberl, K. (2003). Understanding attention: 12- and 18-month-olds know what's new for other persons. *Developmental Psychology, 39*, 906-912.

APPENDIX I

Selection process:

In order to get access to my participants who fit well with my research, I went through a selection process. Through google I searched for South Asian support groups, healthy living centres, Asian community networks and university organisations. I came across several Asian community networks and Asian societies. This online search outlined a list of possible organisations that I could approach for my research.

Nevertheless I had two different target groups (1st generation and 2nd generation), thus I had to undergo a selection criteria in which I put the organisations into three groups. 1) organisations or networks that target the 1st generation; 2) organisations and networks that target the 2nd generation and finally, 3) organisations and networks that target both the 1st and 2nd generation. Furthermore, I arranged the list of organisations and networks in each group in a hierarchy in terms of order of importance (which best fit with my research).

Finally I went through a process of selection and rejection in which I made two lists (organisations and networks for 1st and 2nd generation) of the top of organisations and networks that I was hoping to approach. This process narrowed down my choices, where I was left with two online networks for my 2nd generation (HI5 and Facebook) and 8 for my 1st generation (Asian community counselling services, South Asian counselling services, Hastings all nation support centre, Asian family consultation service, South Asian society, West London Asian society, Asian health agency and Asian resource centre Croydon).

In order to access my 1st generation I found the contact information for each of my organisations and sent an email to the majority with a letter and my research proposal enclosed via the attachment. For those without an email address, I contacted them via phone asking the organisations to mention my study to their clients and ask if they are willing to share their views/thoughts with me. The clients were also told that the online survey would not require much effort from the participants. Also, participating in this study can also be therapeutic for them by allowing them to express themselves anonymously online.

Organisations were told that in return for their time and participation I will give them and their clients 1) acknowledgement for their collaboration; and 2) Co-ownership of the theories and insights generated from this research. In terms of my 2nd generation, participants from HI5 and Facebook were recruited by creating a discussion board group online. The name of my discussion board group was British Asians in London (second generation). As HI5 and Facebook are global networks I had to be precise with my group name. In the discussion board group I outlined the focus of my research project and my website link for the young generation to click on to, in order to participate in my study. I tried to be informal and posted several messages to thank my participants for participating and motivation messages to prompt my participants to participate in the study.

APPENDIX II

First generation:

1) What is stress according to you?

2) How do South Asians perceive stress?

3) Reflect on the changes that you encountered when migrating to this country in terms of:

   a. Social network
   b. Social status
   c. Communication
   d. Values/beliefs and customs

4) From your experience what kind of sources of stress did you go through being migrated from South Asia to Britain? (Please feel free to give some insight on your thoughts and feelings)

5) From your experience what were your sources of stress in the context of family and social dynamics?

6) Do you feel that there is a difference between the way you perceive stress and the second generation in the context of family and social dynamics? (Please feel free to elaborate on your experiences).

7) How do you perceive an 'ideal family'?

8) In comparison to your 'ideal family,' reflect on your relationship with your children?

9) From your experience how does stress affect you:

    a. Behaviour
    b. Attitude towards the way you perceive things
    c. Health status

10) How do you cope with stress?

Second generation:

1) What is stress according to you?

2) From your experience are there any differences between your culture (Asian background) and the Western culture in terms of values, beliefs and traditions?

3) Do you feel that there is a difference between the way you perceive stress and the 1st generation in the context of family and social dynamics?

4) In your opinion what kind of pressures do you face within your family and lifestyle?

5) How do you perceive and 'ideal family?'

6) In comparison to you 'ideal family,' reflect on your relationship with your parents?

7) From your experience how does stress affect your:

    a. Behaviour
    b. Attitude towards the way you perceive things
    c. Health status

8) How do you cope with stress?

APPENDIX III

CONSENT FORM FOR RESEARCH PARTICIPATION

'Cultural perceptions of stress amongst 1st and 2nd generation South Asians in England'

The present study is a requirement for the MSc Health Psychology programme, Department of Psychology, School of Social Sciences, City University.

Your task in this study will consist of participating in an online research survey. You will be required to answer the questions and will be asked to elaborate on your answers with some detail, and you will receive a debriefing slip.

Your participation is completely voluntary and does not involve payment. You are free to withdraw from the study at any time you choose.

This study is not expected to involve risk of discomfort or harm. In the event of discomfort or harm, contact numbers are attached.

To preserve confidentiality the results of this study will be coded in such a way that your identity will not be physically attached to the final data produced.

I have read and understood the above information. I have had an opportunity to ask questions and I have received answers. I consent to participate in this experiment.

APPENDIX IV

Debriefing:

The aim of this study is to demonstrate the understanding of the challenges that can arise from living in two different worlds. This is as the conflict between Asian culture and the British culture can be a source of anxiety for both South Asian parents migrated to Britain and their children who are either born or bought up in the Western nations. This study will look at the sources of stress that Asian individuals from the first and second generation face living in Britain in order to enhance the wellbeing of such individuals.

After data collection, an analysis will be performed. The findings of the analysis will be available on the website.

Please ask if you have any further questions.

Thank you for your participation

Sangeeta Bhalla

Contact details: Sangeeta Bhalla

Email address: *abcj789@city.ac.uk*

APPENDIX V

Phases of thematic analysis:

The stages involved in thematic analysis include the following:

> **First stage**—Researcher familiarises herself with the data

> **Second stage**—Reading and rereading of the text. The researcher comments on his/her first impressions of the text, which include initial thoughts and observation.

> **Third stage**—Identification of initial codes across the data set. The researcher collates the data which is relevant to each code which describes sections of the text. Such codes grasp the quality of what is characterised by the text.

> **Fourth stage**—Searching for themes by clustering the codes identified in stage three into potential themes by looking at the association between one another. The cluster of codes will be given labels, which grasp the fundamental nature of the clustered codes hence gathering all the data which is relevant to each potential theme. Some of these themes will be clustered together whereas others will be illustrated by a hierarchical association with another.

> **Fifth stage**—Review the themes to check if the themes work in relation to the coded accounts and the entire data set.

> **Final stage**—Formation of the report which will include selection of quotations from the accounts to support the codes and themes generated from the data, reflecting back on to the analysis in relation

to the research questions and literature leading to producing a report of the analysis (Braun & Clarke, 2006).

Reflection of my experience when carrying out the thematic analysis:

My experience with thematic analysis as a method of analysis was knowledgeable. This provided me with the opportunity to analyse my participant's accounts with a different approach, than using the usual statistical analysis. Using thematic analysis allowed me to understand and explore the participant's personal experience in depth rather than using a quantitative method which would have summarized the participant's experiences in terms of numerical values. Thematic analysis considers individual differences as it identifies that different factors contribute to the differences in people's personal experiences.

Furthermore, thematic analysis allowed me to be more creative and flexible, hence play an active role in the research. In order to gain an insider's perspective I had to describe, analyse and report patterns within my participant's accounts to make sense of their personal experiences. This allowed me to understand and question my participant's feelings and thoughts regarding their experiences.

Furthermore, the themes which emerged within the data allowed me to sum up the significant features of a large body of data and generated unexpected insight.

Nevertheless, thematic analysis was a challenge as I had never used it before; I had to be careful with what I was doing as I did not want the analysis to be biased with my beliefs. Since the analysis gives the opportunity of flexibility and creativity it was hard to separate my views from my participants, as I had to analyse their experiences thus the analysis had my conceptions of the participant's personal experience. To overcome such barriers *reliability* (the extent to which my measuring procedure yields the same results on repeated trials) and *validity* (the extent to which the method of analysis used is truly measuring what I intended to measure) tests were considered (Heffner, 2004). These included the following:

1) Use of quotations from the participant's accounts to support the codes and themes which were generated from the data

2) Constant comparison—comparing data between and among participant's to see saturation when it happens and also this helps in bringing up gaps in participant's data.

3) Participant's accounts were used to cross validate my findings from the thematic analysis. This was used as conformability to demonstrate the neutrality of the research interpretations.

4) Peer debriefing—Having my South Asian peers review the analysis along the process helped me identify the gaps and discrepancies that I might not otherwise have found. An outsider's perspective often brings other things to light. If the interpretation is similar with others then it improves its credibility (Heffner, 2004).

Overall thematic analysis is a beneficial method as it explores in depth an individuals experience and such human behaviour is difficult to understand in greater depth by using numerical values. However, as thematic analysis is a flexible, creative and time consuming method since you have to re-read through the text several times to capture the essence, as the quality of the participant's account is dependent on the quality of the analysis, many researchers are reluctant to use this. However, thematic analysis presents a more accessible form of analysis for those with limited experience within the qualitative field and is a quick method to learn (Braun & Clarke, 2006).

Effect on the reader:

There was a similarity between the majority of the accounts analysed. The accounts portrayed moving stories regarding the individual's experiences and feelings. Being a South Asian myself I could understand the psychological issues that are raised by both the first and second generation. It was striking to see the changes that the first generation encountered when migrating to England and the tragedies they faced associated with such changes. It made me feel that sometimes the second generation takes what they have for granted. At the same time the second generation feeling that they are torn into both different worlds and experience a confusion of belongingness makes me question the beliefs of the collectivist culture which emphasises 'the concern and need for others.'

APPENDIX VI

First generation responses and individual analysis:

➢ Responses

➢ Analysis

➢ Emerging themes

➢ Summary

Participant 1

"Thu May 10 15:28:23 2007", "Male," "Male (BASAS member)", "India", "26".

"Feeling of being tired and exhausted", "Yes, there are differences between the two cultures. Even after twelve of staying here, I still experience cultural clash." "My social network has LARGELY been confined to the members of the South Asian community." However, I should stress that it does not exclude the member of other national and social backgrounds. Though I have colleagues in the work place from all different national and social backgrounds, my social network still tends to be limited. The social and community gatherings are still dominated by the members of the South Asian community. In other words, it is a home away from home." "My social status back home has enhanced given the fact that I live in the UK. This is largely due to the fact that Indian migration to the West has always been viewed positively and seen to be improving one's socio-economic status (primarily economic status and then associated secondary social status). As my job is respectable here in UK, it has enhanced my social status here as well among certain (educated) segment of the local community." "It has vastly enhanced my communication skills." "My stay in UK has influenced my value system (values, beliefs and customs) to some extend. My value system is still middle-class value system (same in both UK and India). Respect for elders, emphasis on education and ambitions to achieve well in my career, competitiveness are still with me and are being passed on to my family." "My stress was very largely associated with systemic change arisen from the move from one part of the world to another part. Language (pronunciation), behavioural differences (holding the door for others to enter into), financial constraints and the need to face and satisfy the expectations from back home were some elements that caused stress to me." "Yes, the desire to buy a property and compete with fellow members of my social network." "Yes. The elements of my stress are laughable for the members of second generation migrants. Their expectations are again mixed as they are no longer influenced by the social network back home (South Asia). Their stress is related to racism, forced marriages, etc. They display a tendency to resist the pressure put upon them by their parents. However, as a first generation migrant, I was not revolting against my value system (values, beliefs and customs). When they asked me to sit, I knelt down to show that I was a good and well-behaved child to my parents." "My notion of ideal family is the one in which one's imaginative ideals are realised. When I was growing up in India, it was a struggle to survive every day with multiple children in the household with multiple desires." "Yes, I reflect on my past and try to move towards the situation of having an ideal family. I try to maximise the happiness in the household by fulfilling the desires of everyone, including my wife." "It makes me to feel low, dull, lethargic and feel isolated." "It resists my positive attitudes." "I see it's impact as it affects my desire to eat." "Divert the attention and focus on what I like most: playing with my son."

According to participant 1 stress to him is viewed as the feeling of being worn out and feeling isolated and low. He may feel isolated and low due to the limited social network he has in the UK in comparison to the one in India where he first lived. His social network is made up of the South Asian society, hence it is quite limited. Even though the south Asian community is comprised of the minority of the national background he seems to fit in well with those that share the same background as him (South Asians). This is because he feels at home (India—where he migrated from) with them and the community has aspects of the Asian culture. He recognises a difference between the Asian and Western culture in terms of values and customs and says that they still remain even after 12 years, however does not mention any of the differences within the values and customs. He feels that his social status has enhanced back home as they view migrating to the west as improving ones socioeconomic status. Nevertheless such opinions are a source of stress for him, as family back home tends to have further expectations which cause stress. Furthermore, he mentions that he has a good social status in the UK as he has a respectable job being educated. His communication skills tend to be better and I think this could be due to him being exposed to different national backgrounds. Living in the UK has influenced his values to some extent but he still abides to the traditional values which he wants to pass on to his family and children. His sources of stress when he first migrated to the UK were language barriers and the way he behaved due to the values and customs that he was taught back home which he brought with him to the UK. His current sources of stress seem to be meeting the expectations of family back home. He does not signify which expectations but one can assume looking at his account it could be financial matters. As migrating to the west is seen as an improvement in socioeconomic status, family back home may want financial support as they feel he is in the position to or assume that he should be in the position to.

Furthermore he feels that the second generation does not understand the seriousness of the sources of stress that the 1st generation may face. However, he mentions and shows that he has some understanding of the sources of stress that the second generation may have. I feel that he tries to compare the 1st and 2nd generation in terms of abiding to the cultural values that they are born with being from an Asian background. I feel that he thinks that the second generation tends to dismiss that Asian value system and proposes that he would not go against the cultural values and what he is told to do (not voicing his own opinion and respect elders decisions is one of the elements of collectivist culture). He feels that his ideal family is constructed by realising from his previous conditions while he was growing up that he felt it was hard for him to survive in India with a multiple household and children. Participant 1 says he is trying to achieve the ideal, thus I can assume he does not live with extended family but only immediate family with one son. Furthermore, he feels that his ideal family consists of satisfying the needs of his family including his wife. What was striking for me was that the way participant 1 uses his language to mirror the ideal family image. I feel that he seems to provide a metaphoric image of the collectivist culture in India showing the relative status of males and females where males dominate females and there an opinion within matters does not pay such an importance. However, him worrying about satisfying the needs of his wife and stresses the importance if that shows that he is moving away from the collectivist image.

Furthermore, after reading the extract thoroughly line by line I identified the following 16 thematic labels:

Feelings worn out ('feeling of being tired and exhausted') [Line 1].

Culture clash remains after lifetime ('difference between the two cultures . . . . 12 years of staying here') [Lines 1-2].

Restricted social network ('social network has largely been confined . . . . social network still tends to be limited') [Lines 2-6].

Sense of South Asian community in the UK = back home/feeling at home ('social and community gathering . . . . dominated . . . . South Asian community . . . home away from home') [Lines 6-8]

Migration to the west is positively viewed ('Indian migration to the west . . . improving ones socioeconomic status . . . . secondary social status') [Lines 9-12].

Enhanced social status in the UK ('my social status back home has enhanced . . . I live in the UK' and 'As my job is respectable . . . enhanced my social status here as well . . . local community') [Lines 8-9 and 12-13].

Widely held Asian value system amongst 1st generation ('my value system is still middle classed . . . respect for elders, emphasis on education and ambitions . . . passed on to my family') [Lines 15-18].

Systematic change during migration ('stress was largely associated with systematic change . . . language (pronunciation), behavioural differences . . . elements . . . stress to me') [Lines 18-22].

Sources of stress within family dynamics ('the need to face and satisfy the expectations from back home . . . social network') [Lines 22-23].

Sources of stress within Social dynamics ('desire to buy a property and compete with . . . was stress to me') [Lines 23-24].

Lack of understanding ('elements of my stress are laughable . . . second generation migrants') [Lines 24-25].

2nd generation expectations different to back home ('expectation are again mixed . . . no longer influenced by the social network . . . racism, forced marriages . . . resist pressure put upon them by their parents') [Lines 25-28].

First generation still abide cultural values ('first generation migrants . . . not revolting against . . . well behaved child to my parents') [Lines 28-30].

Realisation and improvement from previous struggle ('ideal family is . . . ones imaginative ideals are realised . . . try to maximise the happiness in the household . . . including my wife') [Lines 31-35]

The effects of stress on ones wellbeing ('feels low, dull, lethargic . . . desire to eat') [Lines 35—37]

Change my focus ('divert the attention and focus on what I like most: playing with me son') [Lines 37-38].

Going over the 16 themes that I identified in stage two of the analysis in relation to one another allowed me to construct clusters of themes.

They are as follows: Psychological well-being (themes 1 and 15), Changes encountered during migration (themes 2, 3, 4, 5, 6, 7 and 8), Culture clash (7 and 13), First generation and second generation sources of stress (themes 9, 10, 11 and 12), Family dynamics (theme 14) and Coping method (theme 16).

Psychological well-being		
Feeling worn out	'feeling of being tired and exhausted'	Line 1
The effects of stress on ones well-being	'feels low, dull, lethargic . . . desire to eat.'	Lines 35-37
Coping method		
Change my focus	'divert the attention and focus on what I like most: playing with my son.'	Lines 37-38
Changes encountered during migration		
Culture clash remains after lifetime	'difference between the two cultures . . . . 12 years of staying here'	Lines 1-2 Lines 2-6
Restricted social network	'social network has largely been confined . . . social network still tends to be limited'	Lines 6-8
Sense of South Asian community in the UK = back home/feeling at home		Lines 9-12 Lines 8-9
Migration to the west is positively viewed	'social and community gathering . . . dominated . . . South Asian community . . . home away from home.'	Lines 12-13
Enhanced social status in the UK	'Indian migration to the west . . . improving ones socioeconomic status . . . secondary social status'	
	'my social status back home has enhanced . . . I live in the UK'	
	'As my job is respectable . . . enhanced my social status here as well . . . local community'	

Culture clash Widely held Asian value system First generation still abide to cultural values	'my value system is still middle classed . . . respect for elders, emphasis on education and ambitions . . . passed on to my family' 'first generation migrants . . . not revolting against . . . well behaved child to my parents'	Lines 15-18 Lines 28-30
First and second generation sources of stress Systematic change during migration Sources of stress within family dynamics Sources of stress within social dynamics Lack of understanding	'stress was largely associated with systematic change . . . language (pronunciation), behavioural differences . . . elements . . . stress to me' 'the need to face and satisfy my the expectations from back home . . . was stress to me' 'desire to buy a property and compete with . . . social network' 'stress is related to racism, forced marriages . . . upon them by their parents'	Lines 18-22 Lines 22-23 Lines 23-24 Lines 24-25
2nd generation expectations different to back home	'expectations are again mixed . . . no longer influenced by the social network . . . racism, forced marriages . . . resist the pressure put upon them by their parents'	Lines 25-28

Family dynamics		
Realisation and improvement from previous struggle	'ideal family is . . . ones imaginative ideals are realised . . . try to maximise the happiness in the household . . . including my wife'	Lines 31-35

Overall the summary table shows that living in the UK has been somewhat positive experience for participant 1 in terms of his social status and communication skills. His communication skills have enhanced living within a country with different national backgrounds. Nevertheless his social status as well as being positive is also a source of stress due to family back home. Family back home feel that migrating to the west means gaining socioeconomic status thus may put pressure on participant 1 for matters such as financial support. This stereotypical view may put pressure on him as he may not be or is not always in the position to help the family out financially. This is further supported by participant 1 facing financial constraints. Furthermore, he did face several sources of stress during migration but seems to be getting the best out of it now. However, saying this he still feels a feeling of isolation I feel due to the limited social network he has which is made up of the South Asian society.

Within a collectivist culture sense of community and social support is important thus when he feels stressed living in the UK he may feel isolated. Nevertheless even though he abides to the cultural values he is taught from back home and feels the need for the 2nd generation to respect them, there are certain beliefs that he disagrees with which he has learnt through his past living in India. This is further supported by the notion of his struggles in his past of living in multi-household which he sees as moving away from the ideal family which he has in mind and hence I feel it is moving away from the collectivist family values. If participant 1 has only one son which he only mentions in his accounts shows him disagreeing with having multi-children which is normally expected within an Asian household, thus once again moving away from traditions.

Participant 2

"Wed May 9 14:45:13 2007", "Female," "44," "Bahrain," "27," "Yes, I think the Western culture is far less concerned with keeping the old traditions alive. Whilst they still care as much about each other as we in the Asian culture do, I feel the familial ties are less binding than in our Eastern culture. Too much socialising with the extended family is seen as unhealthy, "sad" even, whilst it is much more a way of life in the Asian culture. A female in the Asian culture will probably put up with an unhappy marriage for far longer than her counterpart in the western culture, because her belief systems are such that marriage is considered sacred.", "My social network decreased significantly coming into this country, but that was to be expected. What was more surprising for me was how hard it was for me as an Asian woman who did not work at the time, to "increase" this social network, in a predominantly white society. Once I started working, this became easier, but still far more difficult than it had been where I came from. Over the years I have adapted more to the Western society and in that I have made myself more "acceptable" to others, and been able to widen my social circles." , "I don't think I felt too much of a change in my social status, except that I was no longer working but rather a wife and a mother to 2 young boys in the first 10 years." , "I did feel a strange disconnection here. I am an educated and quite articulate person, born and brought up in a Middle Eastern country where there were dozens on different nationalities living together. But I did find I could not communicate brilliantly in my early years here. I did not get the British sense of humour, and they certainly did not get mine! I often could not understand them as their English was very slang line and full of regional dialect and accents, something I had not come up against before." , "I am still undergoing the change process in this field. My children are now 16 and 14 years old, and it is through them that I am learning to adapt more to the very different value systems between our two cultures. My children are first and foremost British and very proud to be British—whilst they tolerate my old customs etc they make it very clear that they do not necessarily believe in them. I brought my children up to be independent thinkers, so I cannot now tell them they are wrong! This is what they believe in. The biggest difference between the two cultures in my personal experience is my culture was and still is very much based on ALL OF US, whilst my children belief systems are based on ME ME ME. I don't necessarily think one or other of us is right or wrong—just pointing out that this is the biggest tension in the culture differences debate." , "I think in the early years, I lost my own sense of personal confidence that I had always had taken for granted. Coming into a foreign culture, the same sets of rules applies to friendships, first impressions, humour, etc did not seem to apply. It took a while but I gradually gained my confidence, in the knowledge that I was not superior or inferior to anyone, just different. But the early years were not easy, as being "different" in this country can lead to a kind of "inferiority complex stress". If I, educated and articulate, could feel like this, it would have been much harder for my aunt, who came here 40 years ago, and was not highly educated." , "The constant tension between my own belief systems and my children's belief systems, does sometimes cause some stress to me, but I am learning to deal with this stress in a much more positive manner. I have to learn to not be rigid, and equally I ask my children to try and be more flexible sometimes, particularly when I ask them to do things that involve my parents and the extended family." , "Definitely. The way I was brought up, the "ALL OF US" way, puts a lot of responsibility and expectations on you. You try to please your family, the extended family etc etc. The way my kids look at this is much simpler: do what you want to do, not what you think you should be doing or is expected of you. It sounds so simple but it is not easy to change the way you think overnight." , "An ideal family is close, but not in each other's pockets. They are there for each other in times of happiness and sadness, but should not put too many expectations of each other, because the minute expectations are put on, disappointments tend to follow, with worse. An ideal family should have unconditional love for each other, with the proviso, "this is who and what I am—accept me as I am—and love me as I am." , "I try very hard to get the balance right. Right now my 16 year old is going through a difficult period of hormones/puberty etc, so sometimes the relationship can be a bit stormy, but that is more his age than cultural issues! My relationship with my children is loving, though they do feel sometimes that I expect a lot from them—in terms of grades at school, what chores they should do at home, how much time they should spend with their grandparents! So I listen to them and cut them a bit of slack some of the time, because I know what the expectations can do to people. But on the whole I think my relationship with my children is loving and healthy, with a good dose of the generation gap thrown in!" , "Stress of any sort makes my behaviour very agitated and nervous. It also makes me very angry, and long periods of anger can make my behaviour very strange!", "I have suffered from stress in the last few years, due to a lot of reasons I have already given you—this has in turn made me suffer from IBS—a digestive health problem that has resulted directly from years of stress. I also get stomach ulcers from time to time, although things are much better recently, as I am learning how to deal with stress better." , "I now cope with stress by trying hard to learn what causes me stress in the first place. A lot of my stress was also caused in my workplace, so I have spoken to my colleagues about this and made a lot of changes in the workplace. With my family, I try to cope with stress by sitting down to discuss the problem with my husband and children, and nine times out of ten, we find a solution that reduces my stress as well! I now do regular yoga for the last six years, and that has helped me a lot."

Reading thoroughly through participant 2's account I have found that in terms of the differences between the Western and Asian culture her focus is on the traditional values which show such a difference within the two cultures. I think that the differences that she sees are in terms of family bonding which is closely knitted amongst the Asian culture with immediate and extended. However she mentions that such family ties tend to cause a problem which is a pity as they tend to be the basis of Asian traditional values. She also distinguishes between the Asian and Western culture in terms of the notion of divorce. As within the Asian culture divorce is looked upon especially for females thus within an Asian family a female is more than likely to work on her marriage as holy whereas within the Western nation divorce is common and the best way to deal with the subject matter if marriage is not successful. Furthermore, she describes the changes that she went through when migrating to Britain. In terms of her social network she had many problems. Her social network in Britain was limited as it was hard for her as she was a house wife in India, hence did not work until she came to Britain.

Secondly, migrating to a country with majority Caucasian individuals and not being able to speak fluent English and understand their sense of humour made it hard to increase her social network. It was hard for her to understand them as they spoke in several regional dialects and accents, despite being educated and quite articulated. Thus she felt quite detached from Caucasian individuals. However, gradually she made friends by taking on board some of the western values to gain social acceptance but her social network still remains confined. Being an Asian female who is not allowed to work but nurture her children (traditional value within the Asian culture) was one of the changes in social status that she dealt with.

Furthermore participant 2 feels that she is still constantly adapting herself to the western way of life because of her children as they have been brought up her. Her children seem to agree with the western values and dismiss some parts of the eastern cultural values which she feels is not their fault as she has brought them up to be independent thinkers. In my opinion this is understandable as they are exposed to the western cultural values and have been raised here.

Nevertheless she seems to see a distinction in the way she thinks in comparison to her children. This seems to be her source of stress as her belief system is made up of her cultural values which emphasises on the importance of a sense of community whereas her children's beliefs are based on the notion of independence and hence themselves. She is not saying that her beliefs are right and here children's beliefs are wrong and vice versa but proposes that these cultural differences are debatable. It seems to me that she is trying to bridge the gap between the clashes of thoughts by being less rigid and asking her children to be more flexible especially when concerning their grandparents and extended family as within the Asian culture a lot of importance is given to respecting those that are elder and extended family is viewed just as important as the immediate family.

Moreover, she describes her past sources of stress which was a lack of self-confidence as I think she felt like an outsider at first as what she brought up with in terms of the rules of friendship; first impressions and humour were different to the western nation. Thus she felt at times as inferior however she gained her self-confidence by thinking that she was not below or above anyone she was just different. I think that she gained her self-confidence by self-comparison by making herself feel superior and better by observing the situation of her aunt who had come to this country forty years ago and not being educated whereas participant 2 was educated and came to Britain across a time where there were less acts of discrimination and racism. Also, I think that now her sources of stress tend to revolve around her children having a lack of understanding of their mother's situation.

As participant 2 was brought up with Asian cultural values which include a sense of community which gives rise to responsibility and expectation to please immediate and extended family she cannot disconnect herself from such values over night as they seem to be a part of her, hence will take time. It seems to me that what she does, does not just only affects her but those around her as her life seems to be intertwined with others within her immediate and extended family and this is not her fault as this is the way of life within Asian culture which she is brought up in. Whereas the children's perception of such a situation is based on doing what you want to do and not what you should do. This may sound simple but it is hard to put this into action. I feel that they do not understand the Asian cultural values that she is brought up with.

Furthermore, her perception of an ideal family is the one which behaves as a sense of community but at the same time not being too intertwined in each other's life as this seems to cause conflict due to having expectations and hence being disappointed as it is hard to fulfil them all. She also believes and ideal family should consist of unconditional love thus accepting one for the way they are not the way they should be. Thus I feel she does agree with some parts of what her children believe to do what you want but to some extend as you have to be considerate about those around you. When reflecting on her family she feels that she has a good relationship with her children and feels that there are some problems that she has with her child which is not just only due to culture clash but because of the age that he is 'being a teenager.' Nevertheless like any parent she wants her children to come up with good grades, do the chores in the house and spend some time with their grandparents. However she is not always as rigid as she knows what expectations can do. Thus I feel that she has to deal with several expectations from her immediate and extended family which is the basis of an Asian culture, hence due to this she is quite lenient with her children and hence quite accepting to the western cultural values.

Western culture deals with progressive values ('western culture is far less concerned with keeping the old traditions alive') [Lines 1-2].

Importance of family ('still care as much about each other as we in the Asian culture do . . . familial ties are less binding than in our eastern culture') [Lines 2-4].

Interweaving within extended family viewed unhealthy ('too much socialising with the extended family is seen as unhealthy . . . Asian culture') [Lines 4-5].

Divorce as last option within Asian culture ('a female in the Asian . . . put up with an unhappy marriage for far longer than her counterpart in the western culture because of her beliefs . . . sacred') [Lines 6-8].

Limited social network ('my social network decreased . . . expected') [Lines 8-9].

Status of females with Asian culture ('how hard it was for me as an Asian woman who did not work . . . predominantly white society' and 'no longer working but rather a wife and a mother to 2 young boys in the first 10 years') [Lines 9-11 and 15-16].

Generating social network difficult in the UK comparison to Bahrain ('once I started working, this became easier but still far more difficult than it had been where I came from') [Lines 11-12].

Adapted to western values to gain social acceptance ('have adapted more to the western society in that I have made myself more acceptable to others . . . widened my social circles') [Lines 11-12].

Problems with communication in the UK despite being articulate and educated ('a strange disconnection' and 'I am an educated and quite articulate person . . . not communicate brilliantly . . . not get the British sense of humour, and they certainly did not get mine . . . could not understand them as their English was very slang . . . regional dialect and accents . . . not come against before') [Lines 16-17 and 17-22].

Adapting to western cultural values to meet children's belief system ('still undergoing the change process . . . children 16 and 14 years old, and it is through them that I am learning to adapt more . . . between the two cultures') [Lines 22-25].

Children tolerate eastern cultural values not accept them ('my children are first and foremost British . . . they tolerate my old customs . . . make it clear that they do not necessarily believe in them') [Lines 25-27].

Not at fault for dismissing Eastern values as brought up as independent thinkers ('I brought my children up as independent thinkers so I cannot tell them now that they are wrong this is what they believe in') [Lines 27-28].

Differences in belief systems ('the biggest difference between the two cultures in my personal experience is my culture was as is still very much based on all of us, whilst me children's belief systems are based on me, me, me' and 'constant tension . . . own belief system and my children's belief system') [Lines 28-30 and 40-41].

Cultural difference is debatable ('don't necessarily think one or the other of us is right or wrong . . . biggest tension in the cultural differences debate') [Lines 30-32].

Changes in lifestyle ('lost my own sense of personal confidence . . . the same sets of rules for friendship, first impressions, humour etc did not seem to apply') [Lines 32-35].

Trying to build self-esteem ('gained my self-confidence in the knowledge that I was not superior or inferior to anyone, just different') [Lines 35-36].

Feeling of inferiority ('the early years were not easy as being different in the country can lead to a kind of inferiority complex stress') [Lines 36-38].

Self-comparison ('if I, educated and articulate, could feel like this it would have been much harder for my aunt, who came here 40 years ago, and was not highly educated') [Lines 38-39].

Building a bridge between the generation gap by compromise ('learning to deal with this stress in a much more positive manner . . . learn not to be rigid . . . children try to be flexible sometimes . . . parents and extended family' and 'I listen to them and cut them a bit of slack some of the time, because I know what the expectations can do to people') [Lines 41-44 and 59-60].

Upbringing within Eastern country ('was brought up the all of us way, puts a lot of responsibility . . . expectations on you . . . try to please your family and extended family') [Lines 44-46].

Children go against eastern upbringing ('kids look at this is much simpler: do what you want to do, not what you think you should be doing or is expected of you') [Lines 46-48].

Easily said than done within Asian culture ('it sounds so simple but it is not easy to change the way you think overnight') [Lines 48-49].

Sense of community not intrusion in ones privacy ('an ideal family is close but not in each other's pockets') [Line 49].

Being selfless ('they are there for each other in times of happiness and sadness but should not put too many expectations of each other because . . . disappointment tends to follow, with worse') [Lines 49-52].

Unconditional love ('an ideal family should have unconditional love for each other, with the proviso 'this is who I am—accept me as I am—and love me as I am') [Lines 52-53].

Teenage issues rather than cultural issues ('right now my 16 year old is going through a difficult period of hormones/puberty . . . relationship can be a bit stormy, but that is more his age than cultural issues') [Lines 54-56].

Relationship with children ('my relationship with my children is loving' and 'but on the whole I think my relationship with my children is loving and healthy, with a good dose of the generation gap thrown in') [Line 56 and Lines 60-62].

Expectations from children ('feel sometimes that I expect a lot from them—in terms of grades at school, what chores they should do at home, how much time they should spend with their grandparents') [Lines 57-59].

Effects of stress on behaviour ('stress of any sort makes my behaviour very agitated and nervous. It also makes me very angry, and long periods of anger can make my behaviour very strange') [Lines 62-63].

Effects of stress on health ('I have suffered from stress in the last few years . . . this has in turn made me suffer from IBS—a digestive health problem that has resulted directly from years of stress. I also get stomach ulcers from time to time') [Lines 63-66].

Discussing the problem and taking action ('trying hard to learn what causes me stress in the first place . . . spoken to my

colleagues . . . made a lot of changes in the workplace . . . discuss
the problem with my husband and children, and nine times out of
ten, we find a solution that reduces my stress as well . . . yoga . . .
helped me a lot') [Lines 68-73].

Going over the 31 themes that I identified in stage two of the
analysis in relation to one another allowed me to construct clusters
of themes.

Culture clash (themes 1, 2, 3, 4, 11, 1, 20, 21 and 22), Changes in
migration (themes 5, 6, 7, 8, 9, 10, 15, and 17), Coping method
(themes 16, 18, 19 and 31), Family dynamics (theme 23, 24, 25,
26, 27 and 28) and Psychological well-being (themes 29 and 30).

Culture clash		
Western culture deals with progressive values	'western culture is far less concerned with keeping the old traditions alive'	Lines 1-2
Importance of family	'still care as much about each other as we in the Asian culture do . . . familial ties are less binding than in our eastern culture'	Lines 2-4
Interweaving within extended family viewed unhealthy	'too much socialising with the extended family is seen as unhealthy . . . Asian culture'	Lines 4-5
Divorce as last option within Asian culture	'a female in the Asian . . . . put up an unhappy marriage for far longer than her counterpart in the western culture because of her beliefs . . . sacred'	Lines 6-8
Children tolerate eastern cultural values not accept them	'my children first and foremost British . . . they tolerate my old customs . . . make it clear they do not necessarily believe in them'	Lines 25-27
Not at fault for dismissing eastern values as brought up as independent thinkers	'I brought my children up as independent thinkers so I cannot tell them now that they are wrong this is what they believe in'	Lines 27-28
Differences in belief systems	'the biggest difference between the two cultures in my personal experience is my culture was and is still very much based on all of us, whilst my children's belief systems are based on me, me, me'	Lines 28-30
	'constant tension . . . own belief system and my children's belief system'	Lines 40-41
Cultural difference is debatable	'don't necessarily think one or the other of us is right or wrong . . . biggest tension in the cultural difference debate'	Line 30-32
Upbringing within eastern country	'was brought up the all of us way, puts a lot of responsibility . . . expectations on you . . . try to please your family and extended family'	Lines 44-46
Children go up against eastern upbringing	'kids look at this is much simpler: do what you want to do, not what you think you should be doing or is expected of you'	Lines 46-48
Easily said than done	'it sounds so simple but it is not easy to change the way you think overnight'	Lines 48-49

Changes encountered during migration		
Limited social network	'my social network decreased . . . expected'	Lines 8-9
Status of females with Asian culture	'how hard it was for me as an Asian woman who did not work . . . predominantly white society'	Lines 9-11
	'no longer working but rather a wife and a mother to 2 young boys in the first 10 years'	Lines 15-16
Generating social network difficult in the UK comparison to Bahrain	'once I started working this because easier but still far more difficult than it had been where I came from'	Lines 11-12
Adapted to western values to gain social acceptance	'have adapted more to the western society in that I have made myself more acceptable to others . . . widen my social circles'	Lines 13-14
	'a strange disconnection'	Lines 16-17
Problems with communication in UK despite being articulated and educated	'I am an educated and quite articulate person . . . not communicate brilliantly . . . not get the British sense of humour, and they certainly did not get mine . . . could not understand them as their English was very slang . . . regional dialect and accents . . . not come against before'	Lines 17-22
Adapting to western cultural values to meet children's belief system	'still undergoing the change process . . . children 16 and 14 years old, and it is through them that I am learning to adapt more . . . between the two cultures'	Lines 22-25
Changes in lifestyle	'lost my own sense of personal confidence . . . the same sets of rules for friendship, first impressions, humour etc did not seem to apply'	Lines 32-35
Feeling of inferiority	'the early years were not easy as being different in the country can lead to a kind of inferiority complex stress'	Lines 36-38

Coping methods		
Trying to build self-esteem	'gained my self-confidence in the knowledge that I was not superior or inferior to anyone just different'	Lines 35-36
Self-comparison		Lines 38-39
Building a bridge between the generation gap by compromise	'if I, educated and articulate, could feel like this, it would have been much harder for my aunt who came here 40 years ago, and was not highly educated'	Lines 41-44
		Lines 59-60
Discussing the problem and taking action	'learning to deal with this stress in a much more positive manner . . . learn not to be rigid . . . children try to be flexible sometimes . . . parents and extended family'	Lines 68-73
	'I listen to them and cut them a bit of slack some of the time, because I know what the expectations can do to people'	
	'trying hard to learn what causes me stress in the first place . . . spoken to my colleagues . . . made a lot of changes in the workplace . . . discuss the problem with my husband and children and nine times out of ten, we find a solution that reduces my stress as well . . . yoga . . . helped a lot'	
Family dynamics		
Sense of community not intrusion in ones privacy	'an ideal family is close but not in each other's pockets'	Line 49
		Lines 49-52
Being selfless	'they are there for each other in times of happiness and sadness but should not put too many expectations of each other because . . . disappointment tends to follow, with worse'	Lines 52-53
Unconditional love		
	'an ideal family should have unconditional love for each other, with the proviso "this is who and what I am—accept me as I am—and love me as I am"'	

Teenage issues rather than cultural issues	'right now my 16 year old is going through a difficult period of hormones/ puberty . . . relationship can be a bit stormy, but that is more his age than cultural issues'	Lines 54-56 Line 56
Relationship with children		Line 60-62
Expectations from children	'my relationship with my children is loving'	Lines 57-59
	'but on the whole I think my relationship with my children is loving and healthy, with a good dose of generation gap thrown in'	
	'feel sometimes I expect a lot from them—in terms of grades at school, what chores they should do at home, how much time they should spend with their grandparents'	
Psychological Well-being Effects of stress on behaviour Effects of stress on health	'stress of any sort makes my behaviour agitated and nervous. It also makes me very angry, and long periods of anger can make my behaviour very strange' 'I have suffered from stress in the last few years . . . this has in turn made me suffer from IBS—a digestive health problem that has resulted directly from years of stress. I also get stomach ulcers from time to time'	Lines 62-63 Lines 63-66

Overall her sources of stress arise due to the differences between her children's belief system in comparison to hers. As her belief system is made up of Asian cultural values whereas her children's beliefs are made up of Western values. Such cultural clash is leading to a conflict in thought and views between the two generations and is a cause of her stress today. Whereas earlier her stress was based on her trying to adapt to the western culture while keeping in touch with her traditional values, however now it is her trying to maintain a balance between the western and eastern cultural values because of her children. I feel that they do not seem to help the situation much. This is because they tend to be less accepting towards the eastern cultural values hence disregards some of the beliefs. However through discussion and being able to communicate with the family when problems arise as well as compromise she is able to reduce her stress levels and deal with the situation.

I would like to add by saying that I think that participant 2's children tend to have a lack of understanding regarding the sources of stress their mother went through while migrating to the western nation. Due to this they seem to understand their mother less and hence go against her eastern values. Nevertheless sometimes they do not agree with the Asian customs but bear them for their mother. Whereas the mother having an understanding of both of the worlds is able to understand her children's beliefs better. In comparison the children have a lack of understanding regarding their mother's beliefs as they have only seemed to have seen one of the worlds which they are raised in (western nation). However the children's mother has experienced the differences in both of the cultures (2 different worlds).

Participant 3

"Mon May 14 20:31:52 2007", "Female", "44", "India", "21", "Stress is when there is excessive pressure on my head and when there are so many things on my mind to do where I have limited time to cope with it." , "Asian family is united where people live together and sometimes if you wish to do something you have to get approval from the elders despite being an adult whereas within the western nation they do not live with their extended families and when they turn at the age of 18 they are able to make their own decision as they are seen as adults. Within the Asian cultures females tend to be more reserved than the males as being loud is looked upon. Whereas within the western nation females and males have equal opportunities. In terms of marriage there is no such thing as divorce whereas it is acceptable within the western culture." , "When I came to England I felt isolated and lost, it was a massive change for me in terms of culture and traditions. I had no friends except one who was also an Asian female who had also migrated thus understood how I felt. Gradually after working I got to make more friends within the Asian culture but now as I've lived here 23 years I have made some friends who are not from the same ethnicity." , "My social status has changed. In India after my education which I finished at 20 years of age I got married at the age of 21 as after education that is what happens within Asian families. I got married and come to this country where I was a house wife which was expected as this is what happens within the Asian culture but gradually I started to work which is different to what is expected within the Asian culture." , "Despite being educated within India I had problems with communicating fluently in English as I didn't understand their accent. Therefore sometimes I was too afraid to speak up hence felt socially isolated. But now through my working life I have picked up the English language quite well and may not be perfect at it but am able to speak without hesitation." , "Quite a lot I see males and females as given equal opportunities. I am more open minded with my children where girls are not supposed to talk about matters such as marriage, sex etc I tend to speak about such issues. Obviously sex before marriage is something I am quite strict about still even living in the western nation. But my values and beliefs and way of thinking are still in touch with my Asian values and beliefs such as not having boy friend and girl friends. I believe in arrange marriages as well as love marriages." , "I was away from my family thus did not have much social support, there was a different style and way of living. I didn't do any cooking back home as we had servants but here I had to do everything myself. Here I worked at a saree shop as a sales girl which is looked upon within our family. I had to stand for hours and was taken for granted as I was new and didn't speak much of English. As I did not know how to speak English my colleagues would laugh at me because of my accent, thus I faced discrimination which made me feel more isolated. However, then I got a job as a care worker as they required an Asian female as I spoke several Asian languages. I was then working in the department where I was comfortable as I was working within the Asian community. But now as I have improved as I have been working there since 16 years. I have been promoted as a senior care worker." , "My father in law was very strict despite being married he did not let me share a room with my husband. As he was the head of the house others views within the family were not taken into consideration. I was abused from my father in law as I could not do what I would want. I wasn't allowed to talk to my parents sometimes from back home and they were sometimes told that I wasn't at home even though I was. I was a victim of abuse. I was put under restrictions and felt suffocated. Although my husband had little say because of his father he supported me all the way." , "I want my children to follow the traditional Asian culture although they are born and brought up here. I have financial stress as I have 3 children I need to raise them to settle them down and their future. I feel that my husband sometimes does not spend time with me but goes out of his way to help others. As I wanted my two older children to be bought up they have been however my younger child is a stress for me as she is very much influenced by the western values of doing what she wants to and is exposed to several western values which go against the Asian tradition. Sometimes I have to tell her to respect elders and not argue or raise her voice." , "The second generations stress is parental expectations, importance of education, family being very strict as well as restrictions in terms of going out as this is within the western nation of going out with friends at night and going out till late." , "My ideal family is my children having an understanding of their parents not arguing with their parents and respect. Also share their problems with me. My husband is quite near my ideal who is understanding at times but I tend to have several quarrels with my husband who is always selfless and looks at the needs of others and dismisses my needs sometimes. Although I love my daughter a lot I still do not know how to express myself with her as we lack understanding with each other because I have never had the chance to speak to her properly as I feel she views me in a negative way due to some of the past issues that I haven't mentioned. Recently when she has moved back home from uni we have become closer and talk to her like a friend and hope to express my thoughts regarding the past one day. My son is quite close to me as he didn't go away for further studies, he's caring but he speaks without thinking and has a bad habit which is his smoking which I want to get rid of." , "I want to be alone, I feel angry, sad, low and want to leave everyone and everything and go away." , "I have a negative attitude I'm quiet impulsive and see everyone and everything in the wrong way as I have trouble with viewing what is right and wrong." , "I feel tired, loss of appetite." , "I try to read religious book as I am quite involved in my faith, meditation."

Stress according to participant 3 is not being able to handle too many things at once as this leads to her feeling pressurised, hence feels she does not have the time to cope with it. She describes the Asian family being close knitted and hence decisions that one wants to make is based on the seniors within the family dynamic (which can be comprised of immediate and extended family) despite being an adult. Whereas within the western culture at the age of 18 you are regarded as an adult, hence free to make your own decisions. I think due to this clash between the eastern and western values of being independent and interdependent is where the problem lies. As Asian children are brought up in the western culture society tells them that they are regarded as adults and should be able to make their own decisions at 18 but this opposes the eastern cultural values and causes a conflict as the children find it difficult to decide where they belong.

Furthermore she mentions the difference in the belief system in terms of divorce. Within Asian culture divorce is seen as immoral whereas within the western nation it is widely accepted. She describes her experience when moving to England and the changes that she faced. Such changes were a big shift from what she had been told and the way she was raised. In terms of social network, her social circle became limited and confined as she did not speak the English language fluently she was afraid to speak to her Caucasian counterparts but felt comfortable with individuals from the same ethnicity. However gaining a social circle was difficult for her as she was a house wife at first thus did not have any friends. As she felt comfortable with individuals from the same background she may have accepted a job offer working in a caring home for Asian individuals as she was aware of the languages hence may have felt more comfortable as her English was not so good. She may have accepted the job offer as she felt comfortable as within her previous job she faced discrimination due to the language barriers she had. This was a source of stress for her as she did not know much English she may have not got a well-paid job thus may stress the importance of education to her children and may have expectations from them. This job offer gave her an escape from such sources of stress as she could communicate with people with her mother tongue. Furthermore she describes the change in her social status which was going away from the traditions in which she was brought up in of being a house wife to a working woman. This was moving away from the stages in the life which are already planned coming from an Asian family i.e. after education being married as a housewife, hence maybe showing that there is no different rules for males and females but within the western society they are given equal opportunities. As her own values and beliefs for certain subject matters had changed she raised her children with not the normative strict traditions and values from the Asian culture but was a bit lenient. She raised her children with equal opportunities regardless of being male or female at the same time kept in touch with her Asian values (no sex before marriage, agree with arranged and love marriages, no boyfriend/girlfriend). She may believe in arranged marriages as her marriage despite the ups and downs that she faced is quite successful as she places her family near enough the ideal and seems happy. Also, another change that she faced when migrating to England was lack of social support as she was away from all her relatives and family as well as change in life style.

Despite living in the western nation she lived in a very strict household with her in laws. As the father in law was the senior member of the family house hold what he said mattered whereas others opinions were disregarded. Being brought up with Asian values which are to respect your elders and not to voice any opposing opinion when elders present, may have led her feeling restricted and suffocated. Being isolated and having lack of social support and suffering from abuse from her father in law caused her a lot of stress. Even though the husband acted as a supporting network he did not have much say because of the head of the family. When mentioning her current situation when reflecting on her family there is no reference to her in laws thus may live with just her immediate family, hence her life conditions tend to be better and her family seems to be near her ideal family image. Nevertheless her current sources of stress seem to revolve around her children which is for her children to keep in touch with the Asian cultural values and building a secure future for them, hence may suffer financial constraints. She also feels that her husband does not spend much time with her. This may be as she has a limited social network and feels comfortable with the south Asian community she may want attention from her family members as she is very closely tied to them. She sees her daughter now as a friend and is quite close to her son thus family seems to be an important part in her life and hence may have a limited social life as she feels that she does not need it as she has her family. I think that this is where she misunderstands the situation and may have quarrels with her husband as he may see as well as family life social life is important, hence because of her circumstances she has become quite secluded within a small social network. It may also be that the husband it quite collectivist as he seems to sacrifice his family needs for others which are common within Asian families for extended family due to the past that she has faced from her father in law thus may feel frustrated when her husband goes out of his way to help his father. As within the Asian culture despite the wrong and rights the elders have done, children must always be respectable with their elders.

Participant 3 also stresses about her younger child who is exposed to more western values as she does not want her child to dismiss the Asian cultural beliefs. I feel that participant 3 may view the western culture in a negative way. As there is a clash between her and her daughter's thoughts such as voicing her opinion, arguing and being independent which tend to go with the western cultural values, I think that she misinterprets her daughter's actions by regarding them as westernised due to the image that the western society portrays. Also may have problems with her elder daughter as she may have different views in comparison to her mother as she lived out at university, hence grown more independent than interdependent.

Nevertheless I would like to add that teachings such as respecting elders or think of those around you before doing something as these are common rules that every society within different nationalities and background follow. There seems to be a lack of understanding between the elder mother and daughter as she feels that there seems to be a misunderstanding between them which she is not able to clear as she cannot express herself and does not state this within the text either as it may be personal or she is unable to explain. However she seems to build that relationship and is hoping to have a better understanding with her in which she is able to express to her how she feels.

Furthermore, after reading the extract thoroughly line by line I identified the following 30 thematic labels:

Unable to cope ('stress is when there is excessive pressure . . . so many things on my mind to do . . . limited time to cope with it') [Lines 1-3].

Asian family—close knitted and interdependent ('Asian family is united . . . live together . . . wish to do something . . . get approval . . . from elders despite being adult') [Lines 3-5].

Western family—need of privacy and independence ('Western nation . . . do not live with . . . extended families . . . turn . . . . 18 . . . make their own decisions as they are seen as adults') [Lines 5-7].

Difference in status of males and females within Asian and western culture ('Asian females . . . reserved that the males being loud is looked up . . . western nation female and male have equal opportunities') [Lines 7-9].

Clash in thoughts regarding divorce ('in terms of marriage there is no such thing as divorce whereas it is acceptable within the western culture') [Lines 9-10].

Feeling of being misplaced ('when I came to England . . . felt isolated and lost . . . massive change . . . in terms of culture and tradition') [Lines 10-11].

Limited social network ('I had no friends except one who was also an Asian female') [Lines 11-12].

Comfortable with those from same ethnicity ('Asian female who had also migrated thus understood how I felt . . . more friends within the Asian culture') [Lines 12-14].

In progress of widening social network ('now as I've lived 23 years I have made some friends who are not from the same ethnicity' and 'I was . . . comfortable as I was working within the Asian community') [Lines 14-15 and 37-38].

Change in social status with regards to cultural values ('my social status has changed. In India after my education . . . got married . . . after education that is what happens within Asian families . . . came to this country . . . was a house wife which was expected . . . within the Asian culture but . . . started to work . . . different . . . within the Asian culture') [Lines 15-18].

Problems with communication leading to isolation ('I had problems communicating fluently in English as I didn't understand their accent . . . afraid to speak up . . . socially isolated') [Lines 20-23].

Learning English enhanced self-confidence ('now through working life I have picked up the English language . . . able to speak without hesitation') [Lines 22-24].

Changes in values, beliefs and traditions ('males and females . . . given equal opportunities . . . more open minded with my children . . . speak about such issues') [Lines 24-24].

Still in touch with Asian cultural values ('obviously sex before marriage . . . strict about . . . still in touch with my Asian values and beliefs . . . not having boy friend or girl friends. I believe in arranged marriages as well as love marriages') [Lines 26-30]

Problems during migration ('was away from my family . . . not much social support, there was a different . . . way living . . . worked at a sari shop as a sales girl which is looked upon within our family') [Lines 30-33]

Discrimination ('had to stand for hours . . . was taken for granted as I was new and didn't speak much of English . . . did not know how to speak English my colleagues would laugh at me because of my accent, thus I faced discrimination . . . isolated') [Lines 33-36]

Achievement ('improved . . . promoted as a senior care worker') [Lines 39-40]

Strict father in law ('father in law . . . very strict despite being married he did not let me share a room with my husband') [Lines 40-41]

Status of elders ('as he was the head of the house other views within the family were not taken into consideration' and 'my husband had little say because of his father') [Lines 41-42 and 45-46]

Victim of abuse ('was abused from my father in law as I could not do what I would want. I wasn't allowed to talk to my parents . . .

from back home . . . told that I wasn't at home even though I was. I was a victim of abuse . . . suffocated') [Lines 42-45]

Relationship with husband ('he supported me all the way' and 'my husband is quite near my ideal who is understanding at times but should not think that he is right at all the time') [Lines 46-60]

Raising children ('children to follow the traditional Asian culture . . . financial stress as I have 3 children I need to raise them to settle them down and their future' and 'my younger child is a stress for me as she is very much influenced by the western values of doing what she wants to and is exposed to several western values which go against the Asian tradition . . . voice') [Lines 46-49 and 51-54]

Always in the need to help others ('my husband sometimes does not spend time with me but goes out of his way to help others' and 'several quarrels with my husband who is always selfless and looks at the needs of others and dismisses my needs') [Lines 49-50 and 60-62]

Parental expectation and restriction ('parental expectations, importance of education, family being very strict as well as restrictions . . . going out with friends at night and going out till late') [Lines 54-57]

Ideal relationship with children ('my children having an understanding of their parents not arguing with their parents and respect . . . share their problems and with me') [Lines 57-58]

Relationship with my daughter ('I love my daughter a lot' and 'we have become closer and talk to her like a friend') [Lines 62-63 and 65-66]

Lack of understanding ('I still do not know how to express myself with her as we lack understanding with each other . . . chance to speak to her properly as I feel she views me in a negative way due to some of the past issues that I haven't mentioned') [Lines 62-65]

Hope ('hope to express my thoughts regarding past one day')
[Lines 66-67]

Relationship with son ('my son is quite close to me . . . he's caring
but he speaks without thinking and has a bad habit which is his
smoking which I want to get rid of') [Lines 67-69]

Effects of stress on behaviour ('I want to be alone, I feel angry,
sad, low and want to leave everyone and everything and go away')
[Lines 69-70]

Effects of stress on health ('have a negative attitude I am quite
impulsive and see everyone and everything in the wrong way as
I have trouble with viewing what is right and wrong I feel tired,
loss of appetite') [Lines 70-72]

Spirituality ('I try to read religious book as I am quite involved
in my faith, meditation') [Lines 72-73]

Going over the themes that I identified in stage two of the analysis
in relation to one another allowed me to construct clusters of
themes. They are as follow: first and second generation sources
of stress (themes 1, 16,18, 19, 21, 22, 23 and 26), Culture clash
(themes 2, 3, 4, 5 and 14), changes encountered during migration
(themes 6, 7, 8, 9, 10, 11, 12, 13, 15 and 17), family dynamics
(themes 20, 24, 25 and 28), coping method (themes 27 and 31)
and psychological well-being (themes 29 and 30)

First and second generation sources of stress		
Unable to cope	'stress is when there is excessive pressure . . . so many things on my mind to do . . . limited time to cope with it'	Lines 1-3
Status of elders	'as he was the head of the house others views within the family were not taken into consideration'	Lines 41-42
	'my husband had little say because of his father'	Lines 45-46
Victim of abuse	'was abused from my father in law as I could not do what I would want. I wasn't allowed to talk to my parents . . . from back home . . . told that I wasn't at home even though I was. I was a victim of abuse . . . suffocated'	Lines 42-45
Raising children is a source of stress	'children to follow the traditional Asian culture . . . financial stress as I have 3 children I need to raise them to settle them down and their future'	Lines 46-49
	'my younger child is a stress for me as she is very much influenced by the western values of doing what she wants to and is exposed to several western values which go against the Asian tradition . . . voice'	Lines 51-54
Discrimination	'had to stand for hours . . . was taken for granted as I was new and didn't speak much of English . . . did not know how to speak English my colleagues would laugh at me because of my accent, thus I faced discrimination . . . isolated'	Lines 33-36
Parental expectations and restrictions	'parental expectations, importance of educations, family being very strict as well as restrictions . . . going out with friends at night and going out till late'	Lines 54-57
Lack of understanding	'I still do not know how to express myself with her as we lack understanding with each other . . . chance to speak to her properly as I feel she views me in a negative way due to some of the past issues that I haven't mentioned'	Lines 62-65

Psychological Well-being		
Effects of stress on behaviour	'I want to be alone, I feel angry, sad, low and want to leave everyone and everything and go away'	Lines 69-70
Effects of stress on health	'have a negative attitude I am quite impulsive and see everyone and everything in the wrong way as I have trouble with viewing what is right and wrong I feel tired, loss of appetite'	Lines 70-72
Coping method		
Hope	'hope to express my thoughts regarding the past one day'	Lines 66-67
Spirituality	'I try to read religious book as I am quite involved in my faith, meditation'	Lines 72-73
Culture clash		
Asian family—close knitted and interdependent	'Asian family is united . . . live together . . . wish to do something . . . get approval . . . from elders despite being an adult'	Lines 3-5
Western family—need of privacy and independence	'western nation . . . do not live with . . . extended families . . . turn . . . 18 . . . make their own decisions as they are seen as adults'	Lines 5-7
Difference in status of males and females within Asian and western culture	'Asian females . . . reserved that the males being loud is looked upon . . . western nation female and male have equal opportunities'	Lines 7-9
Clash in thoughts regarding divorce	'in terms of marriage there is no such thing as divorce whereas it is acceptable within the western culture'	Lines 9-10
Still in touch with Asian cultural values	'obviously sex before marriage . . . strict about . . . still in touch with my Asian values and beliefs . . . not having boy friend and girl friends, I believe in arranged marriages as well as love marriages'	Lines 26-30
Always in the need to help others	'my husband sometimes does not spend time with me but goes out of his way to help others'	Lines 49-50
	'several quarrels with my husband who is always selfless and looks at the needs of others and dismisses my needs'	Lines 60-62

Changes encountered during migration		
Feelings of being misplaced	'when I came to England . . . felt isolated and lost . . . massive change . . . in terms of culture and tradition'	Lines 10-11
Limited social network	'I had no friends except one who was also an Asian female'	Lines 11-12
Comfortable with those from same ethnicity	'Asian female who had also migrated thus understood how I felt . . . more friends within the Asian culture'	Lines 12-14
In progress of widening social network	'now as I've lived 23 years I have made some friends who are not from the same ethnicity'	Lines 14-15
Learning English language enhanced self-confidence	'I was . . . comfortable as I was working within the Asian community'	Lines 37-38
Achievement	'now through working life I have picked up the English language . . . able to speak without hesitation'	Lines 22-24
Change in social status with regards to cultural values	'improved . . . promoted as a senior care worker'	Lines 39-40
Changes in values, beliefs and traditions	'my social status has changed. In India after my education . . . got married . . . after education that is what happens within Asian families . . . came to this country . . . was a housewife which was expected . . . within the Asian culture but . . . started to work . . . different . . . within the Asian culture'	Lines 15-18
	'I had problems with communicating fluently in English as I didn't understand their accent . . . afraid to speak up . . . socially isolated'	Lines 20-23
Problems during migration	'males and females . . . given equal opportunities . . . more open minded with my children . . . speak about such issues'	Lines 24-26
	'was away from my family . . . not have much social support, there was a different . . . way living . . . worked at a sari shop as a sales girl which is looked upon within our family'	Lines 30-33

Family dynamics		
Relationship with husband	'he supported me all the way'	Line 46
	'my husband is quite near my idea who is understanding at times but should not think that he is right all the time'	Line 60
Relationship with my daughter	'I love my daughter a lot'	Line 62-63
	'we have become closer and talk to her like a friend'	Lines 65-66
Relationship with son	'my son is quite close to me . . . he's caring but he speaks without thinking and has a bad habit which is his smoking which I want to get rid of'	Lines 67-69
Ideal relationship with children	'my children having an understanding of their parents not arguing with their parents and respect . . . share their problems with me'	Lines 57-58

Overall the summary table illustrates that participant 3 has different sources of stress during the past and now at current. Her source of stress in the past was based on her whereas her source of stress now is based on her children. During the past due to her language barrier she felt isolated and now has a limited social network in comparison to before where she had no friends. I feel that the struggle she went through when getting a job tends to show the importance of education hence for this reason she may stress its importance to her children. Her source of stress at current is regarding her children this is because she is concerned with the culture clash between Asian and western value belief systems.

Furthermore she wants her children to follow her traditional values which seem to be a source of stress for her. One can assume that the sources of stress that she says the second generation faces may be a reflection of the stress that her children may feel they undergo. This is further supported by her image of an ideal family. If this is the case, I think that there is a misunderstanding between the parent and children due to the generation gap. The adapted western cultural values that the parents have absorbed is no longer a stress for the children as they are brought up here they did not face the change in cultural values and beliefs that there parents encountered during migration. Thus may not see this as a source of stress and may overlook it. The sources of stress were more important to just the way these stresses are, but the difference is time. Thus there is a difference in terms of the sources of stress and its importance.

Nevertheless parents may feel that their children have adapted to western values as they go through matters which may have been an issue for them i.e. the social status of males and females being equal was something the parents had to adjust to as it was different from back home in comparison to their children as well as their children being able to openly talk about subject matters which are considered as taboo back home. Thus may feel that their children are lucky to do things which they were not allowed to during their time. Therefore the parents may feel that their children have gained a lot of western values but may forget their own thus stress the importance of Asian traditions and value. However they may not realise that times are changing and there is a generation gap between them hence they may need to understand the importance of their children sources of stress in terms of a change in time.

It is also striking to me the methods that she uses to cope with stress, as she is very much involved with her faith she uses spirituality as a coping method (very traditional, Asian culture—orthodox).

Participant 4

"Tues May 15 22:39:48 2007", "Female", "50", "India", "18", "Stress to me is when I have a lot of pressure from everywhere. I have to do everything and I have no time. When I feel tired and my brain is filled with many things that I can not focus.", "Yes, I feel that everything is openly accepted within western culture where there are several restrictions within the Asian culture. Having sex before marriage is not accepted within Asian culture as well as being in a relationship before marriage. Arguing amongst elders is not accepted whereas it is accepted to say a loud how you feel within western culture.", "I had no friends, felt alone as I was home bound then I slowly started going to work with my aunty where she was a nurse at a hospital but I worked as a domestic cleaner as I was keen to expand on my social network and be able to start communicating with people by learning the English language as I felt frustrated and isolated at home.", "I had only finished my GCSE and used to stay at home and do house chores such as cooking and cleaning. I didn't study further as the females as it is common in Asian culture do not because they get married whereas boys are given more importance as they take on board the family name thus have to be educated. My family also did not have enough money to educate us all as we were too many brothers and sisters within the family, here—working.", "I had a culture shock, I did not even know how to speak in English, when having a medical check when migrating here I could not ask lady to close my buttons of my top at the back, faced many problems with my English language. After working I started learning English through others and now I am not perfect but able to communicate very well with others and have more confidence. I remember I did not know how to use the English toilet as it is different to the one in India.", "Became open minded for my children and understanding as I saw the differences within the culture and did not want my children to face the difficulties as I did. However I am still tied to my Asian roots as I do not believe in sex before marriage, I agree with children having relationship no harm in that but not a girl friend boy friend relationship but as really good friends and like each other as being in a relationship is against Asian culture. Because of this I try to find middle ground as there is a difference in culture.", "I faced language and culture shock. I did not know how to approach white people. I was not confident, felt alone and secluded and did not know what was happening so I felt lost.", "My parents got me married as they wanted me to come here and get settled here as England is privileged because people from back home think we are made of money here and so we are successful. I had no choice as it was my families choice. My aunt lived in the UK so she reassured my mum that she will take care of me. My husband in the UK wanted me to cut ties with my family so I got separated after a lot of struggle. I then lived with my aunty and uncle. My uncle treated me bad and abused me he put several restrictions on me on what I could do and could not do. I went through a divorce at a young age which was difficult as within the Asian culture it is seen as shameful. It was hard being a single female mother as you had many fingers pointed at you from Asian family and friends.", "Now I have financial problems as being a single mother I have to provide for my two children. I am restricted to go out with friends being an adult and do not have my own life as it is dictated by others but before I could not say anything but no as I earn I can have some say and ignore what others say but still have to face them.", "I think they would worry about exams studies, parents restricting them from going out, small things tend to stress them out such as every day problems. They are too sensitive so would not be able to handle things that we went through.", "Having a husband, proper house, being able to go out with family and no tension no back stabbing no hypocrisy within extended family no comparing being nosey, children being understanding and not rebels respecting their parents and not doing what they want to so compromising between both parent and child.", "I have a good relationship with my daughter who is like me. I am firm with my son but do spoil him as he doesn't have a father figure I try to fill in the father space. Kids thinking sometimes do not meet with mine, they have no patience being young and are hot temper which worries me about my daughter as she will be married one day.", "I can think straight, I want to cry and want to be left alone.", "Negative, I tend to jump to conclusions.", "sleep gets affected and I become tired I get headaches and take many paracetamol.", "Talk to my close family members and friends and cry as I feel better."

Participant 4 differentiates between the western and eastern culture in terms their perception of certain subject matters. She feels that the western nation tends to be more open to certain subject matters where the eastern nation is regarded as single mindedness. She describes further that showing the difference between the two cultures in terms of her education. She mentions that she did not study much due to the Asian cultural beliefs of males given more importance to females as the females within the Asian culture are perceived as getting married and ending up as housewives but males are perceived as the breadwinners and hence need to be educated. Therefore I feel when her family had financial constraints as they were not so wealthy, they chose to send their sons to school and may have asked their daughters to give up education.

Furthermore when she describes the changes that she went through during migration, in terms of social network it was limited hence the cause of her feeling isolated as she was home bound. She faced language barriers which made her more isolated from others and it seems that she may have been a sociable person thus was keen to learn the English language to extend her social network. Changes such as culture shock due to the big shift in culture values beliefs and traditions (i.e. change in lifestyle and way of living) she faced a lot of hardship. Through her culture shock she faced isolation as she did not know how to approach her Caucasian counterparts. I can understand the intensity of the isolation that she may have experienced as England during that period when she first migrated was dominated by Caucasian individuals where their was a minority of South Asians whereas now South Asians are the second largest population in England and there is a small difference in terms of percentage in some areas.

As she suffered a lot of difficulty she became broadminded in terms of certain subject matters hence there was a change in some of her cultural values and beliefs as she does not want her children to face the culture clash in which they may have problems fitting in within society. Even though she has tried to maintain her Asian traditional culture values at the same time she has tried to find a balance between the Asian and western culture. She approves of her children being in a relationship with the opposite sex but the way she perceives the term relationship is different in comparison to the western nation. She thinks that it is natural for the opposite sex to have feelings for one another and hence to like each other but being in a relationship as the western nation may portray i.e. moving in with your partner or having sex before marriage.

Moreover she mentions that migrating to the west is much liked by South Asians as they feel that is a way of improving ones socioeconomic status. This is given a lot of importance within the Asian culture as South Asians are very much concerned with sense of community within immediate and extended families, migrating to the west is seen as providing a secure future for one self and their child. This is because Asian cultural traditions are based on parents providing for their children until they are well settled and the children providing for their parents when they are older. It is seen as a sense of duty (dharma). Thus her parents may have been more than happy to get her married to someone in the UK for a secure future for their child.

It seems to me that there is a clash between the ex husband and wife's way of thinking. As it seems to me that he may have been brought up here and may be an independent thinker hence may not have liked the community sense with his in laws as it may have been an invasion of his privacy in terms of his own family household matters whereas her way of thinking may have been different as she came from a collectivist background having rich traditional Asian values as she was raised there. Due to this they may have separated which in turn gave her more suffering as she went against the traditional Asian values of having a divorce. As her values and beliefs changed in terms of divorce her life took a new turning point as she based her decision from what she thought was right from wrong than based on Asian cultural values. Nevertheless she does abide to some of the Asian cultural values. After her separation she moved in with her aunty as she reassured her mum that she would be taken care of. However due to male dominance which is common within Asian culture her aunty did not have much say and could not voice her opinion when she was abused by her uncle.

As mentioned earlier she went against Asian cultural values as she separated from her husband, from then her hurdles started to build up further as she was made to feel ashamed about her actions and had hurtful things said about her at a young age where she was a child herself due to the way of thinking within the Asian culture concerning a lone parent. Now her current sources of stress are based on her children as she has financial constraints being a single mother who wants to provide a secure future for her children as this is the Asian way. Also, it could be that she may not want her children to suffer like she did.

I think that her earning money tends to give her power and some control over her life whereas before she did not have much say. But at the same time I feel that due to the male dominance and the traditional values of the Asian culture which is abiding and respecting elders hence not voicing your opinions she feels that her life has been dictated. Despite participant 4 doing as she desires and disregards others opinions who disagree with her decisions, she still seems to face stress despite having her own say she continues to face problems within her family dynamics (maybe from her uncle arguing or even abusing her as he may feel what she does goes against his wishes).

Furthermore, she recognises the second generations' sources of stress but also mentions that their source of stress is very small in comparison to what she has experienced. Therefore she may see their sources of stress as insignificant as she has gone through worse. Her ideal family seems to be comprised of what she has and what is missing in her life. She feels the need for a husband and a better family household without having family members intertwining within each others house holds. Her reflection of her family at present seems to be her daughter is seen as her friend, hence acts as her social support and fulfils the role if her partner to which she may discuss about her issues and family dynamics. Whereas her relationship with her son is different as she tries to fulfil the missing image of his father by making it up to him thus may spoil him as she does not want her son to feel any different to the other children who have a father figure within their lives.

Also, she feels that her daughter lacks patience and has a hot temper. This seems to worry her as may feel that as she did not have a husband due to the clash of thoughts that they had and seemed to suffer a lot, she wants her daughters marriage to be successful as she feel that her behaviour may be a problem for her in the future when she is married leading to marital conflict.

Furthermore after reading the extract thoroughly line by line I identified the following 32 thematic labels:

1. Pressure with limited resources to cope with ('stress . . . pressure from everywhere. I have to do everything and I have no time . . . brain is filled with many things . . . not focus') [Lines 1-4]
2. Western culture more accepting in comparison to Asian culture ('everything is openly accepted within western culture . . . restrictions within the Asian culture . . . within western culture') [Lines 4-8]
3. Feeling of constraint ('no friends, felt alone as I was home bound') [Lines 8-9]
4. Need for a social network ('slowly started going to work . . . keen to expand on my social network') [Lines 10-12]
5. Defeat isolation ('able to start communicating with people by learning English language as I felt frustrated and isolated at home') [Lines 12-13]
6. Difference in male and female status ('had only finished my GCSE . . . didn't study further as the females . . . do not because they get married whereas boys . . . take on board the family name thus have to be educated') [Lines 13-17]
7. Parent's financial constraints ('my family also did not have enough money to educate us all . . . within the family') [Lines 17-18]

8. Language barriers ('not even know how to speak in English . . . faced many problems with my English language') [Lines 19-21]

9. Improved communication skills ('after working I started learning through others . . . communicate very well with others and have more confidence') [Lines 20-22 and 21-23]

10. Culture shock ('had culture shock' and 'I did not know how to use the English toilet . . . different to the one in India') [Lines 19 and 23-24]

11. Change in values and beliefs for a healthy upbringing ('became open minded for my children and understanding . . . . differences within the culture and did not want my children to face the difficulties as I did') [Lines 24-26]

12. Still in touch with Asian cultural values ('tied to my Asian roots as I do not believe in sex before marriage') [Line 27]

13. Finding middle ground between Asian and western culture ('agree with children having relationship no harm in that but . . . I try to find middle ground as there is a difference in culture') [Lines 27-30]

14. Problems during migration ('faced language and culture shock . . . how to approach white people . . . felt lost') [Lines 31-33]

15. Migrating to west—enhancing socioeconomic status ('parents got me married as they wanted me to come here and get settled here as England is privileged because people from back home think we are made of money here and so we are successful') [Lines 33-35]

16. Decisions made by family members ('no choice as it was my families choice') [Lines 36]

17. Marital conflict ('my husband in the UK wanted me to cut ties with my family so I got separated after a lot of struggle') [Lines 37-38]

18. Feeling limited within social environment ('my uncle treated me bad and abused me he put several restrictions on me on what I could do and could not do') [Lines 39-40]

19. Divorce against Asian cultural values ('I went through a divorce at a young age . . . difficult as within the Asian

culture it is seen shameful . . . many fingers pointed at from Asian family and friends') [Lines 40-43]

20. Financial constraints ('have financial problems as being a single mother I have to provide for my two children') [Lines 43-44]

21. Life dictated by others ('restricted to go out with friends being an adult and do not have my own life as it is dictated by others') [Lines 44-45]

22. Power and control ('now as I earn I can have some say and ignore what others say but still have to face them') [Lines 46-47]

23. Restrictions ('worry about exams studies, parents restricting them from going out . . . we went through') [Lines 47-50]

24. Emptiness ('having a husband, proper house, being able to go out with family and no tension . . . being nosey') [Lines 50-51]

25. Ideal parental and child relationship ('children being understanding and not rebels respecting their parents and not doing what they want to so compromising between both parent and child') [Lines 52-54]

26. Mother and daughter relationship ('I have a good relationship with my daughter who is like my friend' and 'no patience being young and are hot temper . . . worries me about my daughter as she will be married one day') [Lines 54 and 56-58]

27. Playing the role of both mother and father ('am firm with my son but do spoil him as he doesn't have a father figure I try to fill in the father space') [Lines 54-56]

28. Relationship with children ('Kids thinking sometimes do not meet with mine; they have no patience being young and are hot temper') [Lines 56-57]

29. Effects of stress on behaviour ('I can think straight, I want to cry and want to be left alone') [Lines 58-59]

30. Effects of stress on attitude ('negative, I tend to jump to conclusions') [Line 59]

31. Effects of stress on health ('sleep gets affected and I become tired I get headaches and take many paracetamol') [Lines 59-60]

32. Social support and form of release ('talk to my close family members and friends and cry as I feel better') [Lines 60-61]

Going over the themes that I identified 7 clusters in stage two of the analysis in relation to one another allowed me to construct clusters of themes. They are as follows: first and second generation sources of stress (themes 1, 7, 12, 17, 18, 20, 21, 23 and 24), culture clash (themes 2, 6, 16 and 19), changes encountered during migration (themes 3, 4, 5, 8, 9, 10, 11, 14, 15 and 22), coping method (themes 13 and 32), family dynamics (themes 25, 26, 27, 28) and psychological well-being (themes 29, 30 and 31).

First and second generation sources of stress		
Pressure with limited resources to cope with	'stress . . . pressure from everywhere. I have to do everything and I have no time . . . brain is filled with many things . . . not focus'	Lines 1-4
		Lines 17-18
Parent's financial constraints	'my family also did not have enough money to educate us all . . . within the family'	
Marital conflict	'my husband in the UK wanted me to cut ties with my family so I got separated after a lot of struggles'	Lines 37-38
Limited	'my uncle treated me bad and abused me he put several restrictions on me on what I could do and could not do'	Lines 39-40
Divorce against Asian cultural values	'I went through a divorce at a young age . . . difficult as within the Asian culture it is seen shameful . . . many fingers pointed at from Asian family and friends'	Lines 40-43
Financial constraints	'Have financial problems as being a single mother I have to provide for my two children'	Lines 43-44
Life dictated by others	'restricted to go out with friends being an adult and do not have my own life as it is dictated by others'	Lines 44-45
Parental restrictions and education	'worry about exams studies, parents restricting them from going out . . . we went through'	Lines 47-50
Emptiness	'having husband, proper house, being able to go out with family and no tension . . . being nosey'	Lines 50-51
Psychological well-being		
Effects of stress on behaviour	'I can think straight, I want to cry and want to be left alone'	Lines 58-59
Effects of stress on attitude	'negative, I tend to jump to conclusions'	Line 59
Effects of stress on health	'sleep gets affected and I become tired I get headaches and take many paracetamol'	Lines 59-60

Coping method		
Finding middle ground between Asian and western culture	'agree with children having relationship no harm in that but . . . I try to find middle ground as there is a difference in culture'	Lines 27-30
Social support and form of release	'talk to my close family members and friends and cry as I feel better'	Lines 60-61
Culture clash		
Western culture more accepting in comparison to Asian culture	'everything is openly accepted within western culture . . . restrictions within the Asian culture . . . within western culture'	Lines 4-8
Difference in male and female status	'had only finished my GCSE . . . didn't study further as the females . . . do not because they get married whereas boys . . . take on board the family name thus have to be educated'	Lines 13-17
Still in touch with Asian cultural values	'tied to my Asian roots as I do not believe in sex before marriage'	Line 27
Decisions made by family members	'no choice as it was my families choice'	Line 36
Changes encountered during migration		
Feeling of constraint	'no friends, felt alone as I was home bound'	Lines 8-9
Need for social network	'slowly started going to work . . . keen to expand on my social network'	Lines 10-12
Defeat isolation	'able to start communicating with people by learning the English language as I felt frustrated and isolated at home'	Lines 12-13
Language barriers	'not even know how to speak in English . . . faced many problems with my English language'	Lines 19-21

Improved communication skills	'after working I started learning through others . . . communicate very well with others and have more confidence'	Lines 21-23
Culture shock	'had a culture shock'	Line 19
Problems during migration	'I did not know how to use the english toilet . . . different to the one in India'	Lines 23-24
Power and control	'faced language and culture shock . . . how to approach white people . . . felt lost'	Lines 31-33
	'now as I earn I can have some say and ignore what others say but still have to face them'	Lines 46-47
Family dynamics		
Change in values and beliefs for a healthy upbringing	'became open minded for my children and understanding . . . differences within the culture and did not want my children to face the difficulties as I did'	Lines 24-26
Finding middle ground between Asian and western cultures	'agree with children having relationship no harm in that but . . . I try to find middle ground as there is a difference in culture'	Lines 27-30
Relationship with children	'kids thinking sometimes do not meet with mine; they have no patience being young and are hot temper'	Lines 52-54
Mother and daughter relationship	'I have a good relationship with my daughter who is like my friend'	Line 54
	'no patience for being young and are hot temper . . . worries me about my daughter as she will be married one day'	Line 56-58
Playing the role of both mother and father	'am firm with my son but do spoil him as he doesn't have a father figure I try to fill in the father space'	Lines 54-56
Ideal parental and child relationship	'children being understanding and not rebels respecting their parents and not doing what they want to so compromising between both parent and child'	Lines 48-50

Participant 5

"Stress is form of stimulation for the brain. Small stress is good for our brain because it stimulates the brain to carry out the activities but too much stress can be bad for health. In Asian culture there are more family values and family traditions than English culture. In English culture, in most cases children, after the age of 16, like to live independently. Asian families are more bonded together. There are so many ritual ceremonies within Asian culture from birth to death. It is acceptable young couple to live together before marriage in English culture but in Asian culture it is considered very bad. There are a lot of single parents in this country but where as in Asia divorce is very rare. Even if the married couple they don't get on with each other they find ways of compromising to keep the family together. It was very much different initially. The first problem and the main problem I encountered was the language. I could not speak fluent English which straight away put barrier. When I joined school it was very hard for me to make friends. I was isolated in the beginning but later on found few Asian friends who had same circumstances. I had to join English language class to keep up with my language improvement. College was much different because I had been living in the country for some time. English had improved to great deal. I had a lot of confidence. It went uphill since then. My social status had a bit of turbulence through the initial stages of my life. I got married when I was 19 while studying in college. Family circumstances forced me to leave college half way and I did not have enough education to get a good job. At the age of 20, I had my daughter. Life became a bit of struggle. Although I was living with my parents, I had to find job to support my family. My wife was from India and did not have enough education to get good job. Since my daughter was very small it was not possible for my wife to look for job. The pressure was on me. I found job as a sales assistant in a shop. The shop was not the type I would have wanted to pursue my career in but it brought me money. My passion was electronics and wanted to finish my course which I left half way. I joined college in the evenings and it took me four years to finish the course. By then I had my second child. I found job as trainee telecom engineer. It was like dream come true.

Money was not that great but it gave me self-satisfaction because I had come back to electronics field. After working for just 6 months there was another turn in my life. Due to family circumstances I had to go back to India with my family and stayed there for one year. When I came back, I was lucky to go back to the same job. Career started progressing. I changed few jobs and then found job in medical field but still do with electronics. I had my third child. I have been working for the same company and have achieved a lot in my current position. Communication in the beginning was next to zero but as my English improved communication improved too. It was so frustrating in the beginning when I used to be in the class room and teacher asked question. I knew the answer but I was too afraid to answer, in case I pronounced it wrong and the class would make fun of me. When I was small, I was brought up in a very strict environment as my father was very strict. We were not allowed to wear certain clothes. We were not allowed to go to any social events with friends. Father used to dictate the way we were living. While having dinner on the dining table, only father spoke. Our opinions would not count much in the conversation. As I grew up and then got married there were a lot of things that I wanted to experience but never had chance in the past. With due respect our father gave everything to us in terms of the things we needed. I can understand why he was so strict. His father was very strict too. I remember a lot of times he used to quote what his father would say to him when he was small. When my father came to UK, he had the same mentality as his father had. He worked really hard in the beginning and wanted to bring up his children the way his father had taught him. I had different ideas for my children but I had to balance everything. It was difficult but I am very much proud of the way my children are. I did not want my children to be deprived of the way their friend would live but at the same time I had to be a bit firm with them in order to teach them our family traditions. I wanted them to experience both ways of life, English and Asian and get the best of both cultures. I am proud father now. I experienced language barriers, communication difficulties, had a limited social network and experienced difference in culture. Like I explained answer to your question 3, I had very strict upbringing. There were so many things that I wanted to do but because we were afraid to form our opinions because father had only one rule. Things will happen in the house as father says because he was the head of the house. There are different types of stress I had now but I can deal with them in better ways. The main stress as a Asian father is because we are living in an environment where the children are facing two different cultures. English culture is not bad culture. There is more freedom in that culture for youngsters but it is a big challenge to teach your children what they should do and what they shouldn't. In my times, when the dad said no to anything, we did not have any guts to question him because we were too scared of him whereas now if I say no to my children for something, I should have justification for saying no and make sure that the children do not interpret that in a different way. We Asians have come from completely different background to English. We had to learn the English culture at the same time not forgetting our own. We had to build everything from scratch and learnt most of the things hard way. Whereas today, the children a lot of children take things for granted because things are already there for them. The stress in that manner is much more less for them comparing to what we had. They have different stress as they are trying to keep up with their peers. They have a lot of peer pressure, e.g. if their friends are wearing or doing something they would want to keep up with them otherwise they are not part of the same group. We worry about financial security because we have seen hardship is because they have not experienced. My perception of the ideal family is where first of all every member of the family is treated equal. No matter how much work stress or external stress you might have but when you are in the family you have full support of the family to deal with anything comes your way. There is no difference in husband and wife when it comes to doing everyday jobs in the house where in our typical Asian families is wrong. Woman has to do all the house work where man is sitting on his backside resting. There should be equal rights. Every member of the family can form opinion and must be taken seriously. Even if you are the head of the family you must be a good listener. Once any decision has been made, everyone should respect the decision. The most important thing is that everybody should respect each other. Relationship with my children is great. Like I said before that I wanted to bring up my children a bit different the way I was brought up. I have been strict with them when the situation demanded and I have been very easy with them at times. It depends on the stages of the life. When the children are young and they do not have the level of understanding then you have to bit firm to make sure that they do not get in to any mischief. You can't have expectations from children unless you educate them yourself. In order to teach your child, you have to first put yourself in their position and then build them to your level. If at anytime if you have to say no to them for anything, you should have some valid reason and you should explain to the children why you said no. One very important thing I have taught my children, never lie and if you have done something bad be brave to face the consequence. If you are right in whatever you are doing never be intimidated by anyone. Do not be afraid to form your opinion but if you are ever wrong then do not argue. Don't be ashamed to apologise to person even if that person is younger than you. Do not have ego inside you. I have never been in situations before so I am learning as I am going through different stages. Nobody is perfect but you learn a lot of things as you go along. I do jump to conclusions sometime which is not the right thing to do. I get aggressive sometime which again is not the right way of dealing with the things. It depends a lot on the children as well. Some children are more understanding then the others. You have to have different approach with each child to get to the right result. There is a lot of work related stress. I believe you have to learn to live with it. I have become more organised. I have to really control my behaviour with my wife because a lot of the times she can be very provocative. I have improved a lot having positive approach to the situations. I have learnt a lot from my job. There are times when I am wrong badly and I do realise. There is always room for improvement. I have had stroke, so my health has not been that great in the past. It is stress related but touch wood health is ok now. I deal with stress differently than I used to do before. I guess it comes with experience. I think at the end of the day the stress starts from us and finishes with us. It is the way we deal with our daily activities. I have become more organised in doing things. Prioritising my work has helped me a lot."

According to participant 5 stress is healthy when it is in small quantities as it drives the individual to engage in activities whereas excessive amounts of stress is unhealthy. Furthermore, he describes the difference between the western and eastern culture in terms of values and beliefs regarding family dynamic and subject matters such as marriage and divorce. Moreover he feels that the Asian culture is richer in its traditions in comparison to the western culture. During migration participant 5 experienced language barriers therefore felt isolated as this in turn affected his social network which became confined. His social network was based on those who shared similar circumstances to himself. Nevertheless his English language improved as he attended classes where he was taught it. This in turn enhanced his social network and made him confident than isolated. However participant 5 faced several problems in the past as he was married early, he had limited education as he was asked to give it up as he got married and became a father at an early age hence became the only support for his family as his wife was not much educated and had to nurture the child at home. This further affected his ambitions and goals that he set for himself hence sacrificed his ambitions and wishes for the family. He went against his desires and took on board the necessities. It seems to me that he always put his family first before himself, hence his life revolves around his family which is because he is the only form of support that they may have. However later on in his life he was given an opportunity to get closer to his ambition which he took on board despite dealing with financial constraints. As well as experiencing a lot of down falls he was also stepping up the ladder to reach his goal. He faced communication problems when migrated to the UK, he was afraid to voice his opinions amongst his peers in school as he was afraid of what other might think of his accent hence did not want to be an outcast as he already felt isolated. Other reasons for participant 5 not being able to voice his opinion may be due to his father who did not give him an opportunity to formulate his own opinion and say them out loud as he was brought up in a strict manner where his father dictated his life and put several restrictions. This further led him when he got married wanting to do those things which he did not get a chance to because of his father. As he may feel that he is the head of the family thus does not need any authorisation from anyone. Nevertheless he tends to recognise the reason for his father's behaviour which was due to his own upbringing. I feel that participant 5 does not agree with the upbringing that his father gave as he wants to raise his children in a different manner to his father. He does not entirely disregard his father upbringing but wants a balance between a certain amount of restrictions where demanded as well as room for freedom and being able to voice ones opinion. It maybe difficult for participant 5 to raise his children as he has to deal with the culture clash between western and eastern as well as the clash of thoughts with his father. Thus it is difficult to maintain a balance between each of these conditions. He wants to maintain some ties within the Asian culture as well as absorb some western values as he understands the difficulty of fitting in within the western society. Furthermore, participant 5 does not disagree or disregards the western cultural values and does not give the eastern cultural values importance but has formed his values and beliefs by taking out the best of both worlds.

Participant 5's sources of stress in the past were concerned with making adjustments in order to fit in within the western culture as he was born and bought up in India. His major sources of stress when migrating to the UK was language barriers as this gave rise to problems such as communication. This in turn affected his social network leading him to feel isolated. In terms of family dynamics I feel that his main source of stress was his father. As he valued the orthodox traditions, values and beliefs of the Asian culture that he failed to recognise that he will need to change by making adjustments when migrating to the west as their perception of life is dissimilar to his way of life. I feel that he failed to make any of these adjustments and raised his children with the upbringing he had, this led his child to suffer as he was raised with orthodox values but at the same time exposed to the western nation which emphasized the importance of independence, freedom and being able to voice your opinion, hence he found it difficult to adjust with the culture clash.

Due to participant 5 past experience of trying to fit in with the western culture due to the way he was raised with the orthodox

Asian values he decided not to raise his children in that matter as he did not want his children to experience the same struggles as their father. He feels that freedom within the western culture is good however this is a challenge as one needs to draw the line to what extent. This is because too much freedom can cause problems. In comparison to his father he allows his children to raise their own opinion and justifies for his actions of refusal whereas his father did not provide either. Furthermore, he feels that the Asian individuals tend to suffer more than their Caucasian counterparts in terms of stress as they have to keep in touch with their Asian cultural values but at the same time they need to absorb some of the western values to fit in with society. He also compares the 1st and 2nd generation children within the Asian culture and says that the first generation do not have any foundation to make their life whereas the 2nd generation have everything laid out for them which they sometimes tend to take for granted. Furthermore, he feels that the first generations sources of stress were much more stressful in comparison to the second generation. Nevertheless he recognises the differences in the sources of stress between the 1st and 2nd generation. I think that participant 5 feels that the first generation recognises the value of money as they have suffered through a lot of financial hardship whereas the second generation have not experienced this, hence do not realise the value of money.

His idea family concerns equal opportunities, support for each other and a sense of community. He sees no difference in the relative status of male and female. He further does not agree with male dominance and having specified roles within family dynamics regarding stereotypical gender roles, hence equal rights. An ideal family according to him comprises of understanding, respect for each other and being able to voice your opinion.

When he talks about his current family dynamics he seems to be happy with the way he has raised his children as they have been brought up with both sets of cultural values. He has been strict where he is needed to be but at the same time he has been lenient. I think that he has not raised his children in the same way throughout their life but has used a different approach during the life course. For example he was first firm with them when they were at a young age as he needed to teach them right from wrong. Then as the children arrived in their teens he started to become their friend rather than their parent and tried to come down to their level of understanding. It seems to me that participant five has brought his children up in a civil manner where there is a lot of understanding between them. There are several ground rules which are used to gain a healthy relationship between the parent and child. For example, not lying, when wrong face the circumstances, voice your opinion when you feel that something is wrong however at the same time if you're wrong then do not argue. He has learnt a lot from his past experience, hence uses his learning as guidelines for raising his children in a healthy manner.

Participant 5 points out that when he is stressed he behaves in an aggressive manner which he recognises is where he needs to change. He feels that nevertheless certain rules vary for different children as he takes into consideration individual differences. Thus may need to use a different approach when bringing up each of his children. Overall he seems to have a positive approach towards stress and feels that the experience has helped him deal with stress in a different manner with different types of subject matters (i.e. children, work, his wife or himself).

Furthermore after reading the extract thoroughly line by line I identified the following thematic labels:

1   certain degree of stress is healthy lines ('small stress is good for our brain because it stimulates the brain to carry out the activities') Lines 1-2.
2   Excessive stress is unhealthy ('too much stress can be bad for health') Line 2.
3   Asian cultures richer than Western culture ('Asian culture there are more family values and family traditions than English culture') Line 3.
4   Western culture deals with independence ('most cases children, after the age of 16, like to live independently') Line 4.
5   Eastern culture deals with interdependence ('Asian families are more bonded together') Line 5.

6   Differences within Western and Eastern culture in terms of marriage and divorce ('acceptable young couple to live together before marriage in English culture but in Asian culture it is considered very bad . . . in Asia divorce is very rare . . . very much differently initially') Lines 6-10.

7   Language barriers ('the main problem I encountered was the language. I could not speak fluent English which straight away put barrier' and 'join English language class to keep up with my language improvement') Lines 11—12, Lines 14-15.

8   Feeling of isolation ('hard for me to make friends. I was isolated in the beginning but later on found few Asian friends who had same circumstances') Lines 12-14.

9   Gained self-confidence ('Collage was much different . . . English had improved to great deal. I had a lot of confidence. It went uphill since then') 15-17.

10   Turbulence within social status ('my social status had a bit of turbulence through the initial stages of my life') Line 17.

11   Unable to find a balance between marriage and education ('got married when I was 19 while still studying in collage. Family circumstances forced me to leave college half way . . . age of 20, I had my daughter. Life became a bit of struggle') Lines 18-20.

12   Being the only foundation for family support ('living with my parents, I had to find job to support family . . . The pressure was on me') Lines 20-23).

13   Sacrifice ambitions for family ('found a job as a sales assistant in a shop . . . which I left half way') Lines 23-26.

14   Finding a balance between own ambition and necessity ('joined collage in the evenings and it took me four years to finish the course') Lines 26-27.

15   Self-satisfaction more important than wealth ('found job as trainee telecom engineer. It was like dream come true. Money was not that great but it gave me self-satisfaction . . . electronics field') Lines 27-29.

16   Sacrifice for family dynamics ('Due to family circumstances, I had to go to India with my family and stayed there for one year') Lines 30-31.

17 Finally reached his goal which was his ambition ('Career started progressing . . . achieved a lot in my current position') Lines 32-34.

18 Poor communication due to language barriers ('Communication in the beginning was next to zero . . . I pronounced it wrong and the class would make fun of me') Lines 34-38.

19 Strict/restricted/dictated upbringings ('I was brought up in a very strict environment . . . not allowed to go to any social events with the friends. Father used to dictate the way we were living . . . conversation') Lines 38-42.

20 Need for fulfilment ('got married there were a lot of things that I wanted to experience but never had chance in the past') Lines 42-43.

21 Understands the reasons for strict upbringing ('father . . . can understand why he was so strict. His father was very strict too . . . quote what his father would say . . . bring up his children the way his father had taught him') Lines 43-48.

22 Desire to raise children using different approach to fathers ('had different ideas for my children but I had to balance everything . . . not want my children to be deprived . . . had to be a bit firm with them in order to teach them our family traditions') Lines 48-52.

23 Balance between the western an eastern culture ('wanted them to experience both ways of life, English and Asian and get the best of both cultures') Lines 52-53. Difficulties during migration ('experienced language barriers, communication difficulties, had a limited social network and experienced difference in culture') Lines 53-55.

25 Father's rigid beliefs—past source of stress ('very strict up bringing . . . afraid to form our opinions because father had only one rule . . . he was the head of the house') Lines 55-58.

26 Current sources of stress—trying to find a balance between two cultures ('main stress as a Asian father is because we are living in an environment where the children are facing two different cultures . . . big challenge to teach your children what they should do and what they shouldn't') Lines 59-62.

27 Need for justification for refusal ('did not have any guts to question him . . . should have justification for saying no and make sure that the children do not interoperate that in different way' and 'have to say no to them for anything, you should have some valid reason and you should explain to the children why you said no') Lines 63-66, 92-94.

28 Children do not understand the meaning of hardship ('learn the English culture . . . build everything from scratch and learnt most of the things hard way . . . children take things for granted because things are already there for them . . . more less for them comparing to what we had') Lines 67-70.

29 Fitting in within western culture ('different stress as they are trying to keep up with their peers . . . not part of the same group') Lines 70-73.

30 Children do not understand financial hardship ('worry about financial security because we have seen hardship in the past . . . generation what financial hardship is because they have not experienced') Lines 73-75.

31 Equal opportunities ('all every member of the family is treated equal' and 'There is no difference in husband and wife when it comes to doing everyday jobs in the house . . . should be equal rights' Lines 76-77 and lines 79-82.

32 Support ('No matter how much work stress or external stress . . . have full support of the family to deal with anything comes your way') Lines 77-79.

33 Voice opinion ('every member of the family can form opinion and must be taken seriously') Lines 82.

34 Good understanding ('any decision has been made, everyone should respect the decision . . . respect each other') Lines 83-85.

35 Balance between independence and restriction ('bring up my children . . . been strict with them when the situation demanded and I have been very easy with them at times') Lines 86-88.

36 Changes in upbringing with different life stages ('When the children are young . . . not has the level of understanding . . . firm to make sure that they do not get

in to any mischief . . . build them to your level.') Lines 88-92.

37 Honesty ('taught my children, never lie and if you have done something bad be brave to face the consequence') Lines 94-95.

38 Voice your opinion ('If you are right in whatever you are doing never be intimidated by anyone. Do not be afraid to form your opinion') Lines 95-96.

39 Contend yourself when wrong despite being older ('if you are ever wrong then do not argue. Don't be ashamed to apologies to person even if that person is younger than you. Do not have ego inside you') Lines 97-98.

40 Process of learning ('never been in situations before so I am learning as I am going through different stages . . . you go along') Lines 98-100.

41 Effects of stress on behaviour ('jump to conclusions sometime which is not the right thing to do. I get aggressive') Lines 100-102.

42 Different approach in upbringing due to individual difference ('depends a lot on the children . . . different approach with each child to get the right result') Lines 102-104.

43 Everyday stress ('work related stress. I believe you have to learn to live with it') Lines 104-105.

44 Need of control ('really control my behaviour with my wife because a lot of times she can be very provocative') Lines 105-106.

45 Improvement in behaviour ('improved a lot having positive approach to the situations . . . room for improvement') Lines 106-108.

46 Effects of stress on health ('had stroke . . . now') Lines 108-110.

47 prioritizing and being organized ('deal with stress . . . starts from us and finishes with us . . . become more organized in doing things. Prioritizing my work has helped me a lot') Lines 110-113.

Going over the themes I identified 7 clusters in stage two of the analysis in relation to one another allowed me to construct clusters of themes.

They are as follows: Psychological well-being (themes 1, 2, 41 and 46), Culture clash (themes 3, 4, 5, 6, 21, 22 and 23), Changes encountered during migration (themes 7, 8, 9, 10, 11, 12, 13, 14, 15, 16, 17, 18, and 24), First and second generation sources of stress (themes 19, 20, 25, 26, 28, 29, 30, 43 and 44), Family dynamics (themes 27, 36, 37, 38, and 39) and Coping method (themes 32, 33, 34 ,35, 37, 38, 39, 40, 42, 45 and 47).

Psychological well-being		
Certain degree of stress is healthy	'Small stress is good for our brain because it stimulates the brain to carry out the activities'	Lines 1-2
Excessive stress is unhealthy	'too much stress can be bad for health'	Line 2
Effects of stress on behaviour	jump to conclusions sometime which is not the right thing to do. I get aggressive'	Lines 100-102
Everyday stress	'work related stress. I believe you have to learn to live with it'	Lines 104-105
Effects of stress on health	'had stroke . . . now'	Lines 108-110
Coping method		
Support	'No matter how much work stress or external stress . . . have full support of the family to deal with anything comes your way'	Lines 77-79
Voice opinion	'every member of the family can form opinion and must be taken seriously'	Lines 82
Good understanding	'any decision has been made, everyone should respect the decision . . . respect each other'	Lines 83-85
Balance between independence and restriction	'bring up my children . . . been strict with them when the situation demanded and I have been very easy with them at times'	Lines 86-88
Different approach in upbringing due to individual difference	'depends a lot on the children . . . different approach with each child to get the right result'	Lines 102-104
Improvement in behaviour	'improved a lot having positive approach to the situations . . . room for improvement'	Lines 106-108
Prioritizing and being organised	'deal with stress . . . starts from us and finishes with us . . . become more organized in doing things. Prioritizing my work has helped me a lot'	Lines 110-113

Culture clash		
Asian culture more richer than Western culture	'Asian culture there are more family values and family traditions than English'	Line 3
Western culture deals with independence	'most cases children, after the age of 16, like to live independently'	Line 4
Eastern culture deals with western and eastern culture in terms of marriage and divorce	'acceptable young couple to live together before marriage in English culture but in Asian culture it is considered very bad . . . in Asia divorce is very rare . . . very much differently initially'	Lines 6-10
Understanding the reasons for strict upbringing	'father . . . can understand why he was so strict. His father was very strict too . . . quote what his father would say . . . bring up his children the way his father had taught him'	Lines 43-48
Changes encountered during migration		
Language barriers	'the main problem I encountered was the language. I could not speak fluent English which straight away put barrier'	Lines 11-12
	'join English language class to keep up with my language improvement'	Lines 14-15
Feeling of isolation	'hard for me to make friends. I was isolated in the beginning but later on found few Asian friends who had same circumstances'	Lines 12-14
Turbulence within social network	'My social status had a bit of turbulence through the initial stages of my life'	Line 17
Unable to find a balance between marriage and education	'got married when I was 19 while still studying in collage. Family circumstances forced me to leave college half way . . . age of 20, I had my daughter. Life became a bit of struggle'	Lines 18-20
Being the only foundation for family support	'living with my parents, I had to find job to support family . . . The pressure was on me'	Lines 20-23

Sacrifice ambitions for family	'found a job as a sales assistant in a shop . . . which I left half way'	Lines 23-26
Sacrifice for family dynamics	'Due to family circumstances, I had to go to India with my family and stayed there for one year'	Lines 30-31
Poor communication due to language barriers	'Communication in the beginning was next to zero . . . I pronounced it wrong and the class would make fun of me'	Lines 34-38
Difficulties during migration	'experienced language barriers, communication difficulties, had a limited social network and experienced difference in culture'	Lines 53-55
Gained self confidence	'Collage was much different . . . English had improved to great deal. I had a lot of confidence. It went uphill since then'	Lines 15-17
Finding a balance between own ambition and necessity	'joined collage in the evenings and it took me four years to finish the course'	Lines 26-27
Self satisfaction more important than wealth	'found job as trainee telecom engineer. It was like dream come true. Money was not that great but it gave me self-satisfaction . . . electronics field'	Lines27-29
Finally reached his goal which was his ambition	'Career started progressing . . . achieved a lot in my current position'	Lines 32-34
Desire to raise children using different approach to fathers	'had different ideas for my children but I had to balance everything . . . not want my children to be deprived . . . had to be a bit firm with them in order to teach them our family traditions'	Lines 48-52
Balance between the western and eastern culture	'wanted them to experience both ways of life, English and Asian and get the best of both cultures'	Lines 52-53

First and second generation sources of stress		
Strict/restricted/dictated upbringing	'I was brought up in a very strict environment . . . not allowed to go to any social events with the friends. Father used to dictate the way we were living . . . conversation'	Lines 38-42
Need for fulfilment	'got married there were a lot of things that I wanted to experience but never had chance in the past'	Lines 42-43
Father's rigid beliefs-past source of stress	'very strict up bringing . . . afraid to form our opinions because father had only one rule . . . he was the head of the house'	Lines 55-58
Current sources of stress—trying to find a balance between two cultures	'main stress as a Asian father is because we are living in an environment where the children are facing two different cultures . . . big challenge to teach you children what they should do and what they shouldn't'	Lines 59-62
Children don't know the meaning of hardship	'learn the English culture . . . build everything from scratch and learnt most of the things hard way . . . children take things for granted because things are already there for them . . . more less for them comparing to what we had'	Lines 67-70
Children don't understand financial hardship	'worry about financial security because we have seen hardship in the past . . . generation what financial hardship is because they have not experienced'	Lines 73-75
Fitting in with western culture	'different stress as they are trying to keep up with their peers . . . not part of the same group'	Lines 70-73
Need of control	'really control my behaviour with my wife because a lot of times she can be very provocative'	Lines 105-106

Family dynamics		
Need for justification for refusal	'did not have any guts to question him . . . should have justification for saying no and make sure that the children do not interoperate that in different way'	Lines 63-66
	'have to say no to them for anything, you should have some valid reason and you should explain to the children why you said no'	Lines 92-94
Equal opportunities	'all every member of the family is treated equal'	Lines 76-77
	'There is no difference in husband and wife when it comes to doing everyday jobs in the house . . . should be equal rights'	Lines 79-82
Changes in upbringing with different life stages	'When the children are young . . . not have the level of understanding . . . firm to make sure that they do not get in to any mischief . . . build them to your level.'	Lines 88-92
Honesty	'taught my children, never lie and if you have done something bad be brave to face the consequence'	Lines 94-95
Voice your opinion	'If you are right in whatever you are doing never be intimidated by anyone. Do not be afraid to form your opinion'	Lines 95-96
Contend yourself when wrong despite being older	'if you are ever wrong then do not argue. Don't be ashamed to apologies to person even if that person is younger than you. Do not have ego inside you'	Lines 97-98
Process of learning	'never been in situations before so I am learning as I am going through different stages . . . you go along'	Lines 98-100

Participant 6

Tue May 22 16:36:47 2007", "Female", "46 years", "Bengali", "40 years", "Stress is a state of mind that people experience due to any real or perceived danger to their well being. It could be due to an event, situation or thought process. Commonly people talk of stress being the same as anxiety, tension, fear, or worry." "Yes", "When I migrated to UK in 2005, had to seek out the south asian families living in my immediate melieu, and make attempts to make meaningful new friendships with families we could vibe with, so as to provide new avenue for all my family members to socialize with other south Asians", "I felt a stranger amongst the majority white population, this was different when I migrated to Toronto, Canada (2000) as it was a very multi-cultural city of immigrants. Regarding my social status I had to rebuild it once again that was quite challenging and time consuming, as people did not know me or my talents". "I was predominantly speaking in English, (my family joined me after 4 months) and I would yearn to speake in my own languages—Bengali, Marathi and Hindi. Communicating with my relatives and friends abroad (India, Canada USA and others) was very daunting due to limited internet facilities down here in south west UK, and it took a while when I could buy my own computer and eventually get the internet connection". "I had to readjust my values and cutums hugely as the cultural and social environment here is like an 180 degree difference. Especially working as a social worker, I observed that here the threshold of tolerance is quite high, many things are" accepted" as a norm that was in contrast to my own. For e.g drinking from young age and pub culture and having boy/girl friend from age 11/12 or sexual experience from age 13/14 years all these are acceptable as against our Indian culture". I lived in Toronto for 5 years, before coming down to UK. But it was still quite a mitigating period with no support system, and no friends or relative. The stress source was—accommodation, general settlement here (including banking, procuring internet, land/mobile phone, mortgage) and having lived in busy cities like Poona, Bombay and Toronto—the slow pace of life (of course I am now used to this laid back pace and have become part of it)", "Since I came here early to join my work, and the family (2 teenagers and husband) came 4 months later, I became the primary career with huge responsibility of selecting the best schools for my children and take them for admission, help husband towards job search, cooking, shopping, cleaning, maintaining communication with friends and family, and all the mundane DIY jobs for the home. All this with balancing a full time job". "Some times I feel my family is overly dependent on me as a primary carer—the 'mum'—of the house—the guide, the counsellor, the trouble shooter . . . . and it becomes quite overwhelming to get the chores done from them, feed them (Indian cooking preffered—that can be quite time consuming) help them deal with their stressors +I have to deal with the family dynamics of having 2 teenagers in the house . . . . (u know what I mean) etc. With no cook, domestic servant available running a family becomes ery challenging and stressful for a woman, especially if she has a full time job and career aspirations". "Yes. The second generation has to deal with added stressor called as peer pressure. They get caught between the cultural differences of the eastern and western cultures. Also I think the 2nd generation lack patience and become stressful easily". "This is a myth! But of course I think love, care, patience and respect for each other and spending quality time together may be interpreted as essentials for a good healthy family life!" "I think I have built up an excellent relationship with both my children, and am very proud of them. It feels really good when people tell me how well behaved and wonderful person they are and ask me for parenting tips . . . . ;)", "If stressed out I seek to take breaks, rejuvenate myself, so that I can plan the solutions". "I view stress as a challenge, essential part of living and a learning curve. It helps me to be resourceful and perform better". "Prolonged stress may tire me, but no other health problems". "By identifying the source and trying to seek solutions from within and external environment (I am quite resourceful), I also ventilate with my close friends, talk it out, music, dance, laughter, movies, and above all—maintaining a positive attitude and spirituality".

Reading thoroughly through participants 6's account I established that she had not only migrated to the UK from India but also migrated to Toronto in Canada. When she first moved to the UK she used to seek for South Asian families as I think that she may have felt lost and isolated as there was a shift in culture, hence may feel more comfortable with those individuals who share her cultural values and so forth. I think that she wanted to make friends not just acquaintances who may act as a form of support as she migrated on her own, thus did not know anyone else. There was a change in her social status as people were unaware of her abilities. I feel that as she is very much educated being a counselling psychologist she did not face any language barriers but may have been frustrated as she was unable to speak in her own mother tongue. In terms of communication, it was hard for her to communicate with her family who were living in India as she may not have got a well-paid job as it may have been hard for her to settle in the UK, thus she was unable to buy a computer which would have acted as a communication device. Her cultural values changed when she migrated as she saw a shift in the cultural and social environment. She felt that there was a difference in certain subject matters such as dating, sex before marriage and so forth. She faced several sources of stress during migration such as settling herself i.e. need of accommodation, lack of social support and change in lifestyle. As she was the first to migrate to the UK from her family, she became the head of the house. After her family migrated to the UK they became over dependent on her as she was the primary caregiver. (nurturer and exhibited the stereotypical roles of a male). Her family seems to see her as their social support and hence become so over dependent which seems to be her current source of stress. Participant 6 recognises the source of stress that the second generation faces such as peer pressure and culture clash but does not state what types of culture clash or peer pressure. Nevertheless she claims that the second generation lacks patience hence get stressed very quickly whereas the first generation may have a high tolerance. She proposes that an ideal family is a myth however would want there to be love, caring and a sense of community. She describes her relationship with her children as wonderful and gets happy when others praise her children as she feels she has given them the right upbringing. I think that she seems to be a strong character that does not let things get the best of her. She seems to have high tolerance thus does not get stressed easily but views it in a positive way. This is because it helps her perform better and uses positive affect as a coping method where she views the negative image and turns it into a positive image. She lists several coping methods which may be one of the reasons why she may not get stressed easily.

Reading thoroughly through the text line by line I came up with the following themes: Definition of stress ('Stress is a state of mind . . . anxiety, tension, fear, or worry') Lines 1-4.

Gaining a social network (When I migrated to UK in 2005, had to seek out the south asian families living in my immediate melieu.. south Asians') Lines 4-7.

Felling isolated in the UK in comparison to Canada ('felt a stranger amongst the majority white population . . . of immigrants') Lines 8-9.

Rebuilding social status ('my social status I had to rebuild it once again . . . my talents') Lines 10-11.

Hunger to speak in ones mother tongue ('predominantly speaking in English, (My family joined me after 4 months) . . . yearn to speak in my own languages—Bengali, Marathi and Hindi') Lines 11-13.

Lack of communication with relatives abroad ('Communicating with my relatives and friends abroad (India, Canada USA and others) was very daunting . . . get the internet connection') Lines 13-16.

Adjust to cultural values ('had to readjust my values and customs hugely as the cultural and social environment here is like an 180 degree difference') Lines 16-17.

Differences in western and eastern culture ('here the threshold of tolerance is quite high . . . drinking from young age and pub culture and having boy/girl friend from age 11/12 or sexual experience from age 13/14 years all these are acceptable as against our Indian culture') Lines 18-21.

Problems during migration ('accommodation, general settlement here (including banking, procuring internet, land/mobile phone, mortgage) . . . of life') Lines 24-26.

Primary carer Lines ('became the primary career with huge responsibility of selecting the best schools for my children . . . this with balancing a full time job') Lines 28-32.

Interdependent ('feel my family is overly dependent on me as a primary carer . . . having two teenagers in the house') Lines 32-36.

Changes in lifestyle ('With no cook, domestic servant available running a family becomes . . . job and career aspirations') Lines 37-39.

Peer pressure ('The second generation has to deal with added stressor called as peer pressure . . . eastern and western cultures') Lines 39-41.

Lack of tolerance ('2nd generation lack patience and become stressful easily') Line 41.

Healthy family dynamics ('think love, care, patience and respect for each other . . .

healthy family life') Lines 42-44.

Relationship with children ('have built up an excellent relationship with both my children . . . ask me for parenting tips') Lines 44-46.

Take breaks ('seek to take breaks, rejuvenate my self, so that I can plan the solutions' and identify the source and trying to seek solutions from within) Lines 46-47.

Effects of stress on health ('prolonged stress may tire me, but no other health problems') Line 49.

Positive view of stress ('view stress as a challenge, essential part of living . . . perform better') Lines 47-49.

Self-assessment ('external environment . . . maintaining a positive attitude and spirituality ') Lines 50-53.

The themes identified in stage 2 of the analysis share reference points. They are as follows: First and second generation sources of stress (themes 1, 10, 11, 12, 13 and 14), Changes encountered during migration (themes 2, 3, 4, 5, 6, 7 and 9), Culture clash (theme 8), Family dynamics (themes 15 and 16), Coping method (themes 17 and 20) and Psychological well-being (themes 18 and 19).

First and second generation sources of stress		
Definition of stress	'Stress is a state of mind . . . anxiety, tension, fear, or worry'.	Lines 1-4
Primary caregiver	'became the primary career with huge responsibility of selecting the best schools for my children . . . this with balancing a full time job'.	Lines 28-32
Interdependent		Lines 32-36
	'feel my family is overly dependent on me as a primary carer . . . having two teenagers in the house'.	
Changes in lifestyle		Lines 37-39
	'With no cook, domestic servant available running a family becomes . . . job and career aspirations'.	
Peer pressure		Lines 39-41
Lack of tolerance	'second generation has to deal with added stressor called as peer pressure . . . eastern and western cultures'.	Line 41
	'2nd generation lack patience and become stressful easily'.	
Psychological well-being		
Positive view of stress	'view stress as a challenge, essential part of living . . . perform better'.	Lines 47-49
Effects of stress on health	'prolonged stress may tire me, but no other health problems'.	Line 49
Changes encountered during migration		
Gaining a social network	'When I migrated to UK in 2005, had to seek out the south asian families living in my immediate melieu.. south Asians'.	Lines 4-7
Feeling isolated in the UK in comparison to Canada	'felt a stranger amongst the majority white population . . . of immigrants'.	Lines 8-9
Rebuilding social status	'my social status I had to rebuild it once again . . . my talents'.	Lines 10-11

Hunger to speak in ones mother tongue	'predominantly speaking in English, (My family joined me after 4 months) . . . yearn to speak in my own languages—Bengali, Marathi and Hindi'.	Lines 11-13
Lack of communication with relatives abroad	'Communicating with my relatives and friends abroad (India, Canada USA and others) was very daunting . . . get the internet connection'.	Lines 13-16
Adjust to cultural values	'had to readjust my values and cutums hugely as the cultural and social environment here is like an 180 degree difference'.	Lines 16-17
Differences in western and eastern culture	'here the threshold of tolerance is quite high . . . drinking from young age and pub culture and having boy/girl friend from age 11/12 or sexual experience from age 13/14 years all these are acceptable as against our Indian culture'.	Lines 18-21
Problems during migration	' accommodation, general settlement here (including banking, procuring internet, land/mobile phone, mortgage) . . . of life'.	Lines 24-26
Family dynamics		
Ideal family	'think love, care, patience and respect for each other . . . healthy family life'	Lines 42-44
Relationship with children	'have build up an excellent relationship with both my children . . . ask me for parenting tips'.	Lines 44-46
Coping methods		
Take breaks	'seek to take breaks, rejuvenate my self, so that I can plan the solutions'.	Lines 46-47
Self-assessment	'identifying the source and trying to seek solutions from within and external environment . . . maintaining a positive attitude and spirituality'.	Lines 50-53

Participant 7

"Fri Jun 8 10:30:16 2007", "Female", "42", "India", "18", "Stress is when I have a lot of pressure from my inlaws, husband and kids. When I have so much pressure and I can not cope.", 2yes in the asian culture children are ment to respect their elders and concentrate on their education which matters more than being in a relationship. In the western culture children can stop their education at the age of 16 and are allowed to be in relationships. Divorce is also not accepted in the asian culture but in the western culture it is acceptable. In the asian culture smoking is not allowed but it is in the western culture. In the asian culture family is given much more importance than in the western culture and there are many more", "I had no friends but only had one as she came from the same background as me. I didn't speak much to anyone. After I strated work I started making more friends by changing myself to adapt to the western culture so could make gain a social network", "After school I got married and became a house wife now I work at the airport in the duty free shop at Dixons, so I have changed my status as being employed wheeas I was a housewife before.", "I had communication problems as I did not speak much of english apart from the basic words such as hello and how are you and thank you. Then I joined classes to learn english and now I do not have any difficulty and can speak quiet well. My children who speak english most of the time at home have helped me in a way of improving my english language.", "even though I am still religious and spiritual I have changed some aspects of myself in terms of what I wear which is western clothes ather than traditional asian clothes. I still believe in my children having the asian values as I did not smoking, being in a relationship, having a good education and respecting elders however my children have taken on board the western culture which is my biggest stress.", "I faced many challenges as I did not know much english had problems communicating this gave rise to problems for looking for a job as it is hard in the western culture to just having one person working in the family, both partners need to work. I had no friends and my family was back home. The only people that were here were my inlaws and husband who were like strangers as I had an arrange marriage. My inlaws values and beliefs were different as they came from the different part of india to me so we had differences in language and some beliefs.", "My mum was un educated but a great housewife but my dad treated my mum bad and had an affair with another woman despite having 3 children. As my mum was uneducated she did not know tha the papers that she sgned were divorce papers which her husband gave her and took advantage as he was educated. We became dependent on our grandparents as we had no support. As divorce is seen as taboo my father knew that no one would marry me in india so he got me married to someone abroad who were not from the same part of india as us and were different as they were Bengali and I was Indian (hindu).My mum died with cancer at a young age so we became without any support. Me and my brothers became each other's support. They worked and studied and when I got married in London I started working as a domestic cleaner and sent the money I had back home to support my brothers. I had my first child in London who became my life but when he was 5years he died of brain tumour. This was the biggest shock in my life and turned my life upside down. I also had problems with my husband as he was alcoholic he didn't work and everything came upon me I was the provider of the house. My house was repossessed once because of my husband's alcoholic problems.", "Now my husband is getting better but my children are becoming spoilt. During the time I was trying to sort my husband I feel my eldest daughter took advantage of that and started doing things and getting into bad company behind my back. My daughter lft education after gcses which she scraped her passes. She became involved into the western culture of smoking, going around with boys, wearing in appropriate clothing. She argues with me and doesn't treat me as her mum but someone her age that she can shout at rather than respect. I have cried myself to sleep because of her and gone to a counselling psychologists and rang friends asking for advice of how I can control her intollerant behaviour. I have two other younger daughters I do not want them to imitate their elder sister.", "My stress is based on my children whereas their stress is based on themeselves. They thing that their parents are their enemies but do not realise that itis onlyf for their own good. My daughter being educated will do no wonders for me but she will make a better future for herself and not go through the finnancial hardship that ive gone through but have a secure future but they do not realise that. I don't mind her having friends which are boys but I am scared of the things that happen nowadays of girls becomming pregnant at an early age. When will she realise this.", "Good husband, children who have an understanding. A family that understands eachother and supports eachother through thick and thin. Theres love trust and mainly a great understanding!", "My eldest daughter is very disruptive and has no respect for me it doesnt matter how much I do for her she will never realise it till the day I die then she will understand what I said was not wrong. I had no support when young as my mother died my dad left us but when I die I don't want my daughter to beg anyone but stand on her two feet.her being in a bad society will affect her not me.", "I loosed sleep, can not eat and cry alot.", "I start to hate my life and feel that I want to commit suicide but when I think about my children.my attitude is negative.", "went through depression earlier when I suffered through stress.", "I talk to my close friend ask her for advice and this lets me release a heavy baggage which is on my chest. I also pray to God and hope that he can help me get through this struggle."

Reading through participant sevens account it seems to me that her stress tends to revolve around her family dynamics which is comprised of her immediate and extended family. Her source of stress arises from the differences between her and her eldest daughter's views and cultural values to the one they have absorbed. Participant 7 is still in touch with her Asian cultural values but her daughter has grasped the western values which tend to go against the Asian cultural values. Furthermore her current sources of stress are based on the lack of understanding between her and her daughters relationship. Due to the struggles that she has faced as well as those that she has experienced by her own mother of being uneducated, I think that she feels that she does not want her daughter to go through that, hence this may be one of the reasons she gives a lot of importance to education. Also, the repossession of her house may be another reason for her to push her daughter towards education as she wants her daughter to have a secure future and not suffer in terms of financial hardship that she herself went through. Nevertheless she has adapted to the western culture to be socially accepted in society. I think that she may also give more importance to education than relationships due to the hardships that her own mother faced. Participant seven points out the changes she encountered during migration which were language barriers, communication problems, building a social network from scratch, changes in her social status from a house wife to a working woman and so forth.

In terms of relationship, her relationship with her husband seems to have improved as his alcoholic problem was her past source of stress but now she is afraid of the negative relationship that she has with her daughter as she feels that her daughters negative behaviour will reflect on her other children.

Reading line by line through the text I identified the following themes:

1. Excessive pressure ('Stress . . . lot of pressure from my inlaws, husband and kids . . . can not cope.') Lines 1-3.
2. Importance of education and relationship within western and Asian culture ('in the asian culture children are ment to respect their elders . . . the age of 16 and are allowed to be in relationships.') Lines 3-5.
3. Divorce unacceptable within Asian culture in comparison to western culture ('Divorce is also not accepted in the asian culture but in the western culture it is acceptable.') Line 6.
4. Smoking acceptable within Western culture in comparison to Asian ('In the asian culture smoking is not allowed but it is in the western culture.') Line 7.
5. Importance of family dynamics between Asian and western culture ('In the asian culture family is given much more importance than in the western culture.') Lines 7-8.
6. Confined social network ('I had no friends but only had one as she came from the same background as me. I didn't speak much to anyone'.) Lines 9-10.
7. Changed oneself to gain social acceptance ('I started making more friends by changing myself to adapt to the

western culture so could make gain a social network'.)
Lines 10-12.

8. Changes in social status ('became a house wife now I work
    at the airport in the duty free shop at Dixons . . . changed
    my status as being employed wheeas I was a housewife
    before'.) Lines 12-14.

9. Communication problems ('had communication problems
    as I did not speak much of english . . . how are you and
    thank you'.) Lines 14-15.

10. Improving english language ('joined classes to learn
    english . . . helped me in a way of improving my english
    language'.) Lines 16-18.

11. Adapting to western culture at the same time abide to Asian
    cultural values ('still religious and spiritual . . . changed
    some aspects of myself in terms of what I wear which is
    western clothes . . . not smoking, being in a relationship,
    having a good education and respecting elders'.) Lines
    18-21.

12. Children adapting to western cultural values ('my children
    have taken on board the western culture'.) Lines 22.

13. Problems during migration ('faced many challenges as I did
    not know much english had problems communicating . . .
    looking for a job . . . no friends and my family was back
    home'.) Lines 23-26.

14. Confined relationship with in-laws ('only people that were
    here were my inlaws and husband who were like strangers
    as I had an arrange marriage'.) Line 26-27.

15. Differences in beliefs between oneself and in laws ('My
    inlaws values and beliefs were different as they came from
    the different part of india . . . differences in language and
    some beliefs'.) Lines 27-29.

16. Mother faced betrayal from husband ('mum was un
    educated . . . dad treated my mum bad and had an affair
    with another woman . . . mum was uneducated she did
    not know tha the papers that she sgned were divorce papers
    which her husband gave her and took advantage as he was
    educated'.) Lines 29-33.

17. No family support ('became dependent on our grandparents
    as we had no support' and 'mum died with cancer at a

young age so we became without any support'.) Lines 33
and 36-37.

18. Against Asian culture but accepted within western culture
    ('divorce is seen as taboo my father knew that no one
    would marry me in india so he got me married to someone
    abroad . . . (Hindu)'.) Lines 33-36.

19. Siblings each others support network ('Me and my brothers
    became each others support. They worked and studied . . .
    started working as a domestic cleaner and sent the money
    I had back home to support my brothers'.) Lines 37-39.

20. Death of first child (' my first child . . . died of brain
    tumour. This was the biggest shock in my life and turned
    my life upside down'.) Lines 39-41.

21. Alcoholic husband ('had problems with my husband as he
    was alcoholic he didn't work and everything came upon
    me I was the provider of the house'.) Lines 41-43.

22. Repossess house ('house was reposeesed once because of
    my husbands alcoholic problems.'.) Lines 43-44.

23. Daughter associated with bad society ('During the time I
    was trying to sort my husband I feel my eldest daughter
    took advantage of tha . . . into bad company behind my
    back'.) Lines 45-46.

24. Daughter gave less importance to education ('daughter lft
    education after gcses which she scraped her passes'.) Line 47.

25. Daughter against Asian cultural values ('became involved
    into the western culture of smoking, going around with
    boys, wearing in appropriate clothing'.) Line 47.

26. Daughter disregards the relative status of older and younger
    individuals ('She argues with me and doesn't treat me as
    her mum but someone her age that she can shout at rather
    than respect'.) Lines 49-50.

27. Coping strategies to overcome daughters intolerable
    behaviour ('cried myself to sleep because of her and gone
    to a counselling psychologists and rang friends asking for
    advice of how I can control her intollerant behaviour'.)
    Lines 50-52.

28. Fear of younger children imitating eldest daughters
    intolerable behaviour ('have two other younger daughters

I do not want them to imitate their elder sister'.) Lines 52-53.

29. 2nd generation sources of stress based on themselves in comparison to 1st generation ('My stress is based on my children whereas their stress is based on themselves'.) Lines 53-54.

30. Lack of understanding between parent and child ('They thing that their parents are their enemies but do not realise that it is only for their own good . . . becoming pregnant at an early age'.) Lines 54-59.

31. Healthy family dynamics ('Good husband, children who have an understanding. A family that understands each other and supports each other through thick and thin. Theres love trust and mainly a great understanding'.) Lines 59-62.

32. Negative relationship with daughter ('My eldest daughter is very disruptive and has no respect for me . . . not wrong'.) Lines 62-64.

33. Protecting child from struggles she experienced ('had no support when young as my mother died . . . don't want my daughter to beg anyone but stand up on her two feet . . . not me'.) Lines 64-66.

34. Effects of stress on behaviour ('I loose sleep, can not eat and cry a lot'.) Lines 66-67.

35. Effects of stress on attitude ('I start to hate my life and feel that I want to commit suicide but when I think about my children.my attitude is negative'.) Lines 67-68.

36. Effects of stress on health ('went through depression earlier when I suffered through stress'.) Lines 69.

37. Social support ('I talk to my close friend ask her for advice and this lets me release a heavy baggage which is on my chest'.) Lines 69-70.

38. Spirituality ('I also pray to God and hope that he can help me get through this struggle'.) Lines 70-71.

The themes identified in stage 2 of the analysis share reference points. They are as follows:

First generation sources of stress (themes 1, 12, 16, 17, 19, 20, 21, 22, 23, 24, 25, 26, 28, 29, and 30), Culture clash (themes 2, 3, 5, and 18), Changes encountered during migration (themes 6, 7, 8, 9, 10, 11, 13, 14, and 15), Coping method (themes 27, 27 and 38), Family dynamics (themes 31, 32 and 33) and Psychological well-being (themes 34, 35 and 35).

First and second generation sources of stress	'Stress . . . lot of pressure from my inlaws, husband and kids . . . can not cope'.	Line 1-3 Lines 29-33
Excessive pressure		
Mother faced betrayal from husband	'mum was un educated . . . dad treated my mum bad and had an affair with another woman . . . mum was uneducated she did not know tha the papers that she sgned were divorce papers which her husband gave her and took advantage as he was educated'.	Line 33 Lines 36-37
No family support		
	'became dependent on our grandparents as we had no support'	
	'mum died with cancer at a young age so we became without any support'.	
Siblings each others support network	'Me and my brothers became each others support. They worked and studied . . . started working as a domestic cleaner and sent the money I had back home to support my brothers'.	Lines 37-39
Death of first child	'my first child . . . died of brain tumour. This was the biggest shock in my life and turned my life upside down'.	Lines 39-41
Alcoholic husband	'had problems with my husband as he was alcoholic he didn't work and everything came upon me I was the provider of the house'.	Lines 41-43
Repossessed house	'house was repossessed once because of my husbands alcoholic problems'.	Lines 43-44
Daughter associated with bad society	'During the time I was trying to sort my husband I feel my eldest daughter took advantage of tha . . . into bad company behind my back'.	Lines 45-46
Daughter gave less importance to education	'daughter lft education after gcses which she scraped her passes'.	Line 47
Daughter against Asian cultural values	'became involved into the western culture of smoking, going around with boys, wearing in appropriate clothing'.	Lines 47-49

Daughter disregards the relative status of older and younger relatives	'She argues with me and doesn't treat me as her mum but someone her age that she can shout at rather than respect'.	Lines 49-50
Fear of younger children imitating eldest daughters intolerable behaviour	'have two other younger daughters I do not want them to imitate their elder sister'.	Lines 52-53
Lack of understanding between parent and child	'They thing that their parents are their enemies but do not realise that it is only for their own good . . . becoming pregnant at an early age'.	Lines 54-59
\ 2nd generation sources of stress based on themselves in comparison to 1st generation	'My stress is based on my children whereas their stress is based on themselves'.	Lines 53-54
Culture clash		
Importance of education and relationship within western and Asian culture	'in the asian culture children are ment to respect their elders . . . the age of 16 and are allowed to be in relationships'.	Lines 3-5
Divorce unacceptable within Asian culture in comparison to western culture	'Divorce is also not accepted in the asian culture but in the western culture it is acceptable'.	Line 6
Smoking acceptable within Western culture in comparison to Asian	'In the asian culture smoking is not allowed but it is in the western culture'.	Line 7
Importance of family dynamics between Asian and western culture	'In the asian culture family is given much more importance than in the western culture'.	Lines 7-8
Children adapting to western cultural values	'My children have taken on board the western culture'.	Lines 22-23
Against Asian culture but accepted within western culture	'divorce is seen as taboo my father knew that no one would marry me in india so he got me married to someone abroad . . . (Hindu)'.	Lines 33-36

Changes encountered during migration		
Confined social network	('I had no friends but only had one as she came from the same background as me. I didn't speak much to anyone'.	Lines 9-10
Changed oneself to gain social acceptance	'I started making more friends by changing myself to adapt to the western culture so could make gain a social network'.	Lines 10-12
Changes in social status	'became a house wife now I work at the airport in the duty free shop at Dixons . . . changed my status as being employed wheeas I was a housewife before'.	Lines 12-14
Communication problems	'had communication problems as I did not speak much of english . . . how are you and thank you'.	Lines 14-15
Improving English language	'joined classes to learn english . . . helped me in a way of improving my english language'.	Lines 16-18
Adapting to western culture at the same time abide to Asian cultural values	'still religious and spiritual . . . changed some aspects of myself in terms of what I wear which is western clothes . . . not smoking, being in a relationship, having a good education and respecting elders'.	Lines 18-21
Problems during migration	'faced many challenges as I did not know much english had problems communicating . . . looking for a job . . . no friends and my family was back home'.	Lines 23-26
Confined relationship with in-laws	'only people that were here were my inlaws and husband who were like strangers as I had an arrange marriage'.	Lines 26-27
Differences in beliefs between oneself and in laws	'My inlaws values and beliefs were different as they came from the different part of india . . . differences in language and some beliefs'.	Lines 27-29

Coping method		
Coping strategies to overcome daughters intolerable behaviour	'cried myself to sleep because of her and gone to a counselling psychologists and rang friends asking for advice of how I can control her intollerant behaviour'.	Lines 50-52
Social support	'I talk to my close friend ask her for advice and this lets me release a heavy baggage which is on my chest'.	Lines 69-70
Spirituality	'I also pray to God and hope that he can help me get through this struggle'.	Lines 70-71
Family dynamics		
Healthy family dynamics	'Good husband, children who have an understanding. A family that understands each other and supports each other through thick and thin. Theres love trust and mainly a great understanding'.	Lines 59-62
Negative relationship with daughter	'My eldest daughter is very disruptive and has no respect for me . . . not wrong'.	Lines 62-64
Protecting child from struggles she experienced	'had no support when young as my mother died . . . don't want my daughter to beg anyone but stand up on her two feet . . . not me'.	Lines 64-65
Psychological well-being		
Effects of stress on behaviour	' I loose sleep, can not eat and cry a lot'.	Lines 66-67
Effects of stress on attitude	'I start to hate my life and feel that I want to commit suicide but when I think about my children.my attitude is negative'.	Lines 67-69
Effects of stress on health	'went through depression earlier when I suffered through stress'.	Lines 68-69

Lightning Source UK Ltd.
Milton Keynes UK
UKOW04f1357060915

258135UK00001B/100/P